Stress Control

Stress Control

How You Can Find Relief From Life's Daily Stress

Steve Bell

SkillPath Publications

Mission, Kansas

Project Editor: Kelly Scanlon

Editor: Jane Doyle Guthrie

Page Layout and Cover Design: Rod Hankins

ISBN: 1-57294-053-0

Library of Congress Card Catalog: 96-68882

10   9   8   7   6   5   4   3   2   99   00

Printed in the United States of America

Contents

Preface

This book is written simply and straight to the point. Designed only to help you bring the stress in your life under control before the consequences are *out* of control, it's not meant to substitute for professional help. If you even suspect that stress has caused you some serious illness, make an appointment to see your doctor and get treatment as soon as possible. The same advice applies if stress has stretched you to near the emotional breaking point. If that's the case, you need to talk with a qualified mental health professional. Your doctor or a member of the clergy may be able to help you find such a resource.

On the other hand, if the symptoms associated with your stress are milder, or if you're already being treated for a stress-related condition, this book is for you! The goal is not to try to make you a medical expert or to qualify you to give professional advice on stress; the only intent is to provide the information essential to releasing you from its power.

Stress Control was not meant to be read in one sitting and then put away, though it's short enough the average reader could easily do so. It was written to be an interactive resource, and it's filled with exercises and things you can do to *un*stress. As a matter of fact, those are the most important parts. Controlling stress isn't a matter of reading or knowing. It's a matter of doing! Let's get started.

Chapter One

Let's Get Started

Most books on stress begin with explanations of what the phenomenon is and how it affects you physically and mentally. Though this book will cover those things, you're going to start off in a different way—and for a reason: If you're feeling stressed, you want some relief as soon as possible.

Consider the techniques in this chapter "Band-Aids" or "timeouts." Practice them and you're on your way to managing stress. "On the way" because there's much more to unstressing your life than what's offered in this preliminary fashion. Still, it's hard to concentrate on what you need to know to become the stress-free person you want to be when you're all tensed up and strung out.

One of the first keys to getting rid of the tense feelings of stress is to take control of your breathing. When you're stressed, your breathing may become shallow, or you may even hold your breath for short periods of time. Some people tend to hyperventilate instead. Whatever your personal breathing pattern when you tense up, one thing is for sure—you're not getting the correct amount of oxygen for your body's optimal operation. Relax your breathing and you'll begin to relax everything else too. This is the first step in controlling the effects of stress.

Read the following exercise instructions and give deep breathing a try. It isn't important to do it perfectly the first time—every time you practice this simple technique, you'll get better at it. The first several times it will help if you reread the instructions and see if you're leaving out any part of them. Every little bit helps!

Timeout #1
Deep Breathing Exercise

1. Practice deep breathing in a sitting position. It may be easier to relax when you're lying down, but there aren't that many places to lie down during the workday. You want to get good at relaxing in a position that's convenient and practical when you need it—when you're feeling stressed. A comfortable chair is a help, but the only really important thing is that wherever you're sitting is comfortable.

2. As you sit, close your eyes and squirm around a little. Stretch the muscles in your neck, your shoulders, and the trunk of your body a little by moving around gently in place. Tilt your head slowly from one side to the other. Don't force it. Just give your muscles a chance to relax.

3. Next, sit up straight in a position in which you feel balanced. If you're in a chair with a back to it, and it's fairly comfortable, you'll want to scoot your hips all the way against the backrest and lean back until you feel support. If your seat has no back, you can achieve a balanced position by leaning the trunk of your body forward, just slightly.

4. When you feel in balance, facing straight to the front with your eyes closed, let your shoulders relax more. You will feel them "lengthen" or "widen."

5. Take a deep breath, preferably through your nose, and let it out with a sigh. As you do, let your shoulders relax even more. As the air is expelled, don't slump over. Stay upright and balanced.

6. Continue to breathe slowly and easily for a minute or two—at least fifteen or twenty breaths. As you breathe in, let your abdomen expand. Don't puff up your chest as you inhale. Each time you exhale, relax more deeply. Concentrate on your breathing. Make it natural, not forced.

Let's Get Started

7. At the end of a minute or two, open your eyes and go on with whatever you were doing before you started your timeout from stress.

Practice this relaxation exercise whenever you feel yourself tensing up and want some relief from that tension. However, remember that although deep breathing is probably the most widely recommended tension-relieving technique, it's by no means the only one. Maybe you'd like an alternative to use once in awhile. Maybe you're one of those people who find vigorous activity more relaxing than just sitting there. If so, try the next technique instead.

Timeout #2
Brief, Brisk Exercise

1. Jog in place for a minute or two—until you feel your pulse rate begin to quicken, or if you're really into fitness, do ten or twelve push-ups or sit-ups.

2. After the period of brief exercise, stretch a little, then stand or sit until your breathing has returned to normal rate for a minute or so. (See, you're back to natural breathing again!)

A minute or two of brisk exercise also helps eliminate the neurochemicals that build up with tension. Some people find it's more effective than deep breathing when they're angry as well as when they're stressed. And, getting into some physical activity can have a paradoxical effect. If you're feeling hyperenergetic, it can have a calming effect: if you're tired when you start, the activity can give you more pep.

If you spend a lot of time in an environment where sitting with your eyes closed or bouncing around in exercise could be misinterpreted, following is another variation that involves brisk walking.

Timeout #3
Secret Mission

When you feel the stress mounting, simply pick up a bunch of papers, or a file folder, or some object you use at work, and silently decide on a "secret mission" to take that object somewhere and bring it back. The reason for carrying something is to make you appear busy so no one will be likely to interrupt. The reason for calling it a secret mission is that the way you walk needs to be brisk and purposeful, and the round-trip should take at least two or three minutes. Walk as if you're on an important mission, in somewhat of a hurry, and get those arms swinging. It might not be as vigorous as a dozen push-ups, but this exercise will release tension and help you breath more naturally when it's over.

Part of the benefit of any timeouts from stress is that they do what the name implies: They give you some time away from whatever you're experiencing as stressful. They take your mind off what's troubling you. Another strategy to relieve the effects of stress is to simply take a timeout from working and do something that will occupy your mind in a positive way. Many people like to build some of these breaks into the day, whether they're feeling particularly stressed or not. A timeout also can help *prevent* feelings of stress. Following are some examples of short timeouts.

Timeout #4
Just Take Time Out

1. Take a short walk and just enjoy the scenery.

2. Read a chapter in a daily meditations book.

3. Call a friend and have a short conversation about something pleasant.

4. Browse at a nearby shopping center.

5. Read from one of your favorite magazines.

6. Go someplace private and sing a song.

7. Go someplace in public and sing a song.

8. Jog or do a short workout.

9. Draw a pencil sketch.

10. Crochet or do needlepoint.

11. Write a poem.

12. Plan a surprise for someone you love.

The possibilities are endless—limited only by your own creativity. Getting away from stressors, even for just a few minutes, can make a big difference in your energy level and productivity. With the boost the timeouts will give you, you'll be ready to get on with your total stress-control program. So, now that you have at least some temporary relief from stress, let's start at square one and find out what stress is all about.

Chapter Two

Stress and Your Life

Linda is off work today. Her ulcer is acting up again.

Jamal is in the hospital recovering from a heart attack.

Maria has been having her excruciating headaches more and more often.

Phyllis has been drinking more lately. She doesn't have a major alcohol problem yet, but she can hardly wait for cocktail hour so she can relax.

Nguyen is just plain pooped, and doesn't care whether he gets his work done or not.

All these people are suffering from the same thing—stress. Chances are, you are too, or you wouldn't have picked up this book. If you think stress is getting to you, please keep on reading—for your own sake. Stress not only makes you tired; it can be a killer. It kills productivity, careers, relationships, and happiness. Yes, stress even kills people.

Among the illnesses that have been linked to stress in medical studies are high blood pressure, heart attacks, strokes, indigestion, ulcers, colitis, menstrual disorders, depression, psychotic episodes, muscle spasms, backaches, drug dependence, alcoholism, arthritis, bursitis, sexual dysfunctions, and susceptibility to colds and flu. Some researchers even suggest a link between stress and cancer.

It's been estimated that 50 percent or more of all people who consult a doctor are there for an illness related, at least in part, to stress. Stress weakens the immune system. It can make you sick, make you think you're sick, or make you worse if you're already sick.

You've probably seen many articles on stress and physical health. You also may have come across the Holmes-Rahe stress inventory, which lists stressful situations and assigns them point values. The points represent how strongly that situation has been associated with stress-related illness. The high point value items are not a surprise—death of a spouse, divorce, marital separation, a jail term, death of a close family member or a serious personal injury or illness—but some items on the list are not what you'd expect: getting married, buying a home, experiencing an outstanding personal achievement, getting promoted at work. Without stress management, it seems, just about any life change can cause stress.

Another often-published list ranks occupations in terms of stress. You can consult such a list and assess whether your type of job is one in which people seem to "let it get to them." The problem with both the "stressful situation" and the "stressful job" approaches to measuring the stress in your life is that some people are able to manage situations and jobs that are highly stressful for others, while some may become highly stressed out by events another person may handle with only moderate difficulty.

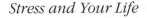

Research has identified certain personality traits and habits that make people stress-prone. These include attributes like being a "people pleaser," being highly critical of yourself and others, denying yourself relaxation and pleasure, and tending to take on too many responsibilities. If you have these traits, you keep your mental and physical system "revved up" a great deal of the time and become a likely candidate for the harmful effects of stress.

The bottom-line question is—how much is stress affecting you right now? The following questionnaire will help you find out.

Stress and Your Life

STRESS TEST

Answer each item "true" or "false," as it applies to you:

T   F

- ☐ ☐ I feel too tired to really work effectively or enjoy my hobbies a good deal of the time.
- ☐ ☐ I am late for work or for appointments at least once a week.
- ☐ ☐ I often feel sad, depressed, or bored.
- ☐ ☐ I used to be more interested in sex.
- ☐ ☐ I am working longer and harder and not making any headway.
- ☐ ☐ I am frequently irritable, impatient, grumpy, or short-tempered.
- ☐ ☐ I wish I could return to the happier days that used to be.
- ☐ ☐ I have frequent headaches, muscle spasms, stomach or intestinal trouble, or high blood pressure, or have gained or lost weight without wanting to.
- ☐ ☐ It is hard to find time for personal and social activities.
- ☐ ☐ I have a relationship that is troubling me.
- ☐ ☐ I have to force myself to go to work . . . or to go home.
- ☐ ☐ I am hanging on to a job or relationship because I feel I have no other alternative.
- ☐ ☐ I am drinking more than I used to (or smoking or using legal/illegal drugs more).
- ☐ ☐ I often wish I were somewhere else.
- ☐ ☐ There have been too many changes in my life lately.

☐ ☐ I am under pressure to succeed all the time.

☐ ☐ I am unable to relax without drugs or alcohol.

☐ ☐ I have lost sight of my life's dream.

☐ ☐ I take myself and the way other sees me very seriously.

☐ ☐ I must push on and keep my nose to the grindstone.

No. of True ___ No. of False ___

Give yourself one point for each "true" answer, and then compare your score to the analysis below.

0-5 • "Cool under fire." You report handling stress well and staying calm. Check your answers just to make sure you weren't minimizing some difficulties in your life.

6-10 • "In the frying pan." You are feeling stressed, and could become a candidate for a stress-related illness.

11-15 • "In the fire." The flames of burnout have begun. Stress is already taking its toll.

16-20 • "Burnt." You are approaching the "flame-out" stage. Stress threatens your career, health, and relationships.

No matter how you scored, whether you were "cool under fire" or "burnt," read on! If you already manage stress well, this book can make your good life even better. If you're in the "burnout" stages, these pages can change your life in a truly dramatic way.

In the next chapter, you'll learn what causes stress and what it can do to you. You'll also identify the sources of stress in your life, which is the first step toward real stress control.

Chapter Three

Stress Is Everywhere

In one sense, you can't get away from stress—there's just no such thing as a stress-free environment. At the most peaceful mountain lake, for example, there's likely a park ranger worried to distraction about the chance of a forest fire or a resort owner wringing his hands over seasonal occupancy rates. At the most gorgeous sun-drenched beach, some tourist is probably suffering through a major case of sunburn and another's mind is churning with business problems that are hundreds of miles away.

These examples make it clear, though, that the stress that gets to you may or may not be in an external event. Most often, actually, the stress that sickens or kills is in you and your reactions to outside events. Those reactions are both mental and physical.

The ancient Greeks came to conceive of the mind and the body as separate entities. Everything could be classified as either one or the other—period. That way of looking at things was accepted for a long time. About a hundred years ago, however, psychologist William James and his colleagues began to debate the mind-body connection. If you saw a bear in the woods, did you run because you felt fear, or did you feel fear because your reaction was to run?

Modern research proves that some of each is true. Our thoughts can stimulate the flow of hormones and neurotransmitters that are associated with particular emotional states. On the other hand, when our physical systems are aroused, our minds interpret our internal condition in terms of an emotion or feeling.

The meaning we attach to our immediate situation may determine what label we put on the emotion. Sometimes this leads to what social psychologists call *misattribution*. One variation on this is the "Romeo and Juliet effect." According to misattribution theory, those ill-fated lovers interpreted the combined excitement of their attraction plus the tension of doing something their feuding parents would not approve of as the passion of an absolutely irresistible love. Their fear and infatuation added up to major excitement, which they interpreted as overwhelming love because of the immediate situation—two young people alone on a balcony.

The same kind of misattribution explains why you feel grumpy with everyone when you're stressed. The mind attaches your internal condition (angry) to whatever situation you happen to be in. Emotions can be confusing and hard to label.

A clue to both the complexity of labeling our feelings and how stress works on us lies in the word "excitement." Hans Selye, considered the father of stress management, defined stress in terms of the excitement of certain body processes and systems. As a biologist, Selye was quite interested in discovering what processes led to aging, illness, and death—the "wearing out" of the organism. He found that high levels of physical excitement, which he called the *alarm reaction*, led to specific physical changes. These included enlargement of the adrenal glands, shrinking of the thymus, atrophy of the lymph nodes, and ulcers in the stomach.

Selye described the process related to these changes as the *general adaptation syndrome.* There are three phases of the GAS process. In the first, the "alarm phase," your brain alerts your body to gear up for stress. Everything is thrown into a maximum energy condition. During the "resistance" phase, your body continues to operate at this stepped-up pace to resist or cope with the stress. If you remain in the resistance phase for longer than your physical systems can tolerate, you enter the "exhaustion phase"—your resources are depleted and you collapse in exhaustion, or even death.

The course of the general adaptation syndrome is essentially the same as what we call the "fight or flight" syndrome. When faced with a threat, our bodies mobilize—heightening blood circulation to the major muscles of the arms and legs that are used in fighting and running. You know the sensation—your heart rate speeds up, your breathing becomes rapid, and your nervous system pumps out epinepherines. (Most of us call this "adrenaline," but that's actually the name of the synthetic, man-made version.) You are primed to survive! At this point, your body operates under the control of the *sympathetic nervous system*, one of two neurological "programs" built into human physiology.

When you're relaxed and not under threat, the other program kicks in: the *parasympathetic nervous system.* In this state, your breathing and heart rates slow, and more blood circulation is available for coordinating fine–motor skills, digesting your food, and engaging in sexual activity. (If the Romeo and Juliet example seems to conflict with the explanation of the two major programs of our nervous systems, consider this: The instinctive courtship displays of birds and animals usually include elements of both mating and territory-defending behaviors. Bonding seems to involve some aspects of overcoming fear in many species.)

Stress Is Everywhere

The two systems, or programs, cannot be active at once—it's either fight-flight or relaxation. When it comes to how all this affects us physically and can make us sick, it is simply that our bodies can't run "supercharged" for long periods of time. The sympathetic nervous system's fight-flight response had great survival value when our ancestors had to protect themselves from wild animals and warriors from hostile tribes. In the modern world, it doesn't always serve us as well. Also, it's possible for your "throttle to get stuck," so to speak, resulting in exhaustion and depletion of physical resources.

A dramatic example of this seems to occur in victims of post-traumatic stress disorder (PTSD). PTSD sufferers are victims of long-lasting stress reactions due to unusually stressful events, such as combat, natural disasters, or being an object of violence. Studies of these people show that changes occur in brain structure and output of certain hormones and neurotransmitters. These changes may be so dramatic that they never reverse themselves. One part of the brain that seems to react to this prolonged stress reaction is the *hippocampus* (Latin for "sea horse," which describes the shape of this brain area). Post-traumatic stress victims have been found to have enlarged hippocampi, which may account in part for their difficulty concentrating, nervousness, and volatile emotions.

Medicines, at least the ones available today, are not very effective at bringing our nervous systems back from the effects of stress. Most drugs that encourage relaxation require increasingly stronger doses to remain effective. They become physically and/or psychologically addictive. The mind-body combination seems to be constantly trying to readjust itself to the premedication level of arousal.

Also, drugs tend to have a "backlash" effect. When you take synthetic compounds to achieve a particular physical state, your body tends to stop producing the natural substance that creates the same end. As a result, when you discontinue the medication, you're at least temporarily worse off than before. An example is alcohol, a central nervous system depressant that some people use to calm down when they're stressed. If the dose is sufficient, or if a person uses the "beverage tranquilizer" over a long period of time, the body tries to counteract the effect and bring things back to the person's "normal" excited condition. When the alcohol wears off, the person thus feels tense and irritable as part of the hangover. This is partly the consequence of alcohol's toxic effect and partly the product of the body's overcompensation.

Perhaps not surprisingly, the best chemicals for counteracting the effects of stress are natural ones that your body manufactures. One example of these is a group of neurotransmitters called *beta-endorphins*. These operate like natural pain killers and tranquilizers. When internal levels of beta-endorphins are high, you can endure more stress and more pain. You can increase your beta-endorphin output by doing two things—exercising and laughing. That's why getting exercise and exercising your sense of humor are parts of all good stress management programs.

The point of all of this is that to be free from the physical and mental symptoms of stress, you must be healthy in mind and body. A healthy body encourages a healthy mind. A healthy mind gives the body a chance to do its natural thing and stay healthy.

A final note on the mind part of the mind-body combination: Despite the fact that things we consider positive events are included on lists of stress factors in our lives, they are not nearly as exhausting as our "negative" stressors. In fact, Hans Selye found that stress in moderation can offer some mental and physical benefit. He concluded that a goal of avoiding all stress is unrealistic and unproductive. The stress we are trying to avoid, he pointed out, is purposeless stress, particularly that associated with fear and anger. This type he called *DIStress*.

A life totally free of stress would be dull and uninteresting. Who would want to live without contests, roller coaster rides, weddings, celebrations, and exciting vacations? The fact is that people who are in normal, good physical health almost never become seriously ill from "good stress." Oh, you've probably had the experience of

Stress Is Everywhere

overdoing it a bit and catching a cold or the flu. Once in a great while, you may hear of someone who was in poor health having a stroke or heart attack after some joyful excitement. But have you ever heard of someone in their prime, healthy years dying of a stress-related illness caused by too many wonderful, thrilling, joyful experiences? No, the killer stress is DIStress.

Through some quirk of human nature, distressful feelings seem to last longer than pleasant ones. The phenomenon can be a "vicious circle" reaction within the mind-body system. Your mind perceives a threat, and your body reacts. You grow consciously aware then of a change in the way you feel physically, and that reminds you to think the distressful thought again. As it goes round and round, you become trapped in worry, ongoing anxiety, or resentment. The origins of the latter word even imply this process—to repeat the same "sentiment," to have the same feeling over and over again. Positive stress comes and goes with the events that generate it; the negative variety tends to just hang on.

With this understanding of what stress is and how it affects you, it's time to analyze the stressors in your life. Exercise 1 will get you started.

Exercise 1:
Identifying Your Stressors

First, list the situations in your life that are sources of positive stresses. Then note the sources of your DIStress. Don't try to evaluate them or figure out what to do about them yet—just list them. Some examples are provided to get you started.

My sources of positive stress:

    1. *My children*

    2. *My new job*

    3. *My continuing education classes*

    4. *My exercise/workout program*

    5. *Performing in the church choir, going to rehearsals*

    6. *Walking the dog*

My sources of negative stress (DIStress):

    1. *My children—when they misbehave*

    2. *Worry about meeting or missing deadlines*

    3. *My hot-tempered, demanding boss*

    4. *The high cost of living—too many bills*

    5. *The failing health of my parents*

    6. *All the road construction going on that costs me precious time*

    7. *Exams and term papers*

You may have more or fewer persons, things, or situations on your positive and negative stressors lists than appear in the examples. You may have many minor or moderate stressors, or only a few very big ones, or some combination of both. Whatever stressors appear on your lists, the important thing is to get them written down. This is your start on controlling stress in your life.

Stress Is Everywhere

My positive stressors are:

1. _____
2. _____
3. _____
4. _____
5. _____
6. _____
7. _____
8. _____
9. _____
10. _____

My negative stressors are:

1. _____
2. _____
3. _____
4. _____
5. _____
6. _____
7. _____
8. _____
9. _____
10. _____

You probably didn't think of all your positive and negative stressors on your first try, though you no doubt remembered the most important ones. As you think of other items later, add them to your lists. Forgotten stressors may continue to pop into your mind for several days, as you are reminded during day-to-day activities. In the meantime, keep moving ahead. The next chapter will start working on the machine that has to carry your stress load—your body.

Chapter Four

Stress and Your Body

"How long you think that you can run that body down?"

This line from a Paul Simon song could become the theme song for stress control, in more ways than one. When we allow emotional stress to rule, we run our bodies down. When we literally abuse our bodies and don't keep ourselves physically healthy, we are setting ourselves up for stress-related illnesses.

A bonus of a healthy body is that it encourages a healthy attitude and more resistance to emotional stress. Keeping your body healthy and stress-resistant means eating the proper foods, avoiding excesses and other unhealthy habits, exercising to stay fit, and getting sufficient rest. Maybe you've heard and read about preventive maintenance for your body. But are you practicing what you know about good health? Read on and decide for yourself how well (or badly) you're treating yourself.

Are You What You Eat?

If what you eat is healthful, you're likely to stay healthy. If what you eat not healthful, you'll eventually become unhealthy. Maybe a more accurate revision of the old cliché would be: "Healthy or unhealthy, we BECOME what we eat!" Just as your car needs the proper fuel to keep it from banging and chugging along or even conking out, your body needs the correct fuel to keep it running right.

Actually, there are few foods that are so bad for you that you should never eat them (unless an allergy or medical condition dictates what your diet should be). The real problem is lack of balance in nutrition. And maybe the information on a balanced diet isn't as available as you might think.

For many years, we were bombarded with information on "the four food groups" (later revised to five groups). But in the late 1980s, nutritionists at the U.S. Department of Agriculture added a new twist. To stay healthy, they noted, wasn't just a matter of getting some food from each group each week; the key lay in *how much*. A new nutritional grouping concept was born: the food pyramid. You've probably heard of it, maybe even read an article on it or seen it on the side of your cereal box. However, it's surprising how slowly the concept has caught on.

Contrary to what you might expect, the average neighborhood public library may not have even one book that explains this major new system of analyzing nutrition. There are many books on diets— diets for heart patients and diabetics, diets for athletes and fitness buffs, diets for the overweight and the underweight as well. Many of them contain accurate and useful information on healthy menus, but few emphasize the real concept behind the food pyramid. Let's look at this simple way of analyzing your diet.

The Food Pyramid For Balanced Nutrition

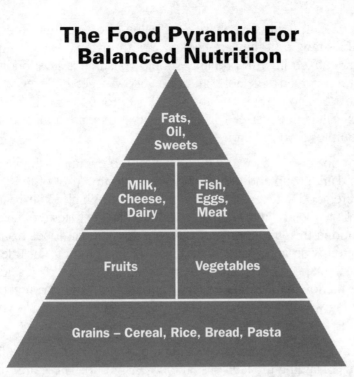

Note how the area of the triangle occupied by each level becomes successively smaller from bottom to top. The amount of space represents approximately the portion of your diet that you should draw from foods in that area.

At the broad base of the pyramid lies the largest group—grains—which includes items such as bread, cereal, rice, and pasta. The emphasis here is on foods like whole-grain breads and cereals that aren't full of or covered with sugar. These foods tend to be high in fiber and low in fat. As the mainstay of human nutrition, you should include something from this group in virtually every meal.

Next, above the grains in the pyramid, appear the fruit and vegetable groups. These foods are also vital to good nutrition. A good deal of our vitamin and mineral requirements come from these foods. Beans, for example, offer excellent sources of protein, and citrus fruits are excellent sources of vitamin C, an immune system enhancer. Nutritionists emphasize the value of eating fruits and vegetables raw, or if they are cooked, not throwing away the liquid they are cooked in. You probably should consume at least one type of fruit, one green vegetable, and one yellow vegetable every day. Note that the fruit group and the vegetable group are of approximately equal size. This indicates that they are about equally important to good nutrition.

Two groups also occupy the third level of the pyramid—the milk-cheese-dairy group and the fish-eggs-meat group. Most of these foods are good sources of protein, but many are high in fat content. Most of the dietary items that lead to high blood cholesterol levels are found in this group. It's not essential that you eat foods from these groups on an everyday basis, yet you may tend to include them as a major part of almost every meal. Worse, you may seldom opt for the low-fat, low-cholesterol options here. And if you choose something with lower fat content, such as chicken or fish, do you boost the fat content by frying?

At the top of the pyramid, occupying the smallest space, is the little triangle containing the fats, oils, and sweets group. These are basically nonessential to good health. At best, they represent "empty calories," devoid of vitamin, mineral, or protein benefits, but they're not automatically bad for you. In modest quantities, fats, oils, and sweets are not harmful to a healthy person. There may even be some benefit to including some oils and fats in your diet. The problem again comes with overdoing it. Reliance on fried foods, greasy sauces and dressings, quick-sugar-fix snacks, and sweetener-laden cereals is characteristic of inhabitants of the wealthiest countries on Earth.

Our dietary habits have their price. Because of all the sweets, oils, and fats, America has the highest percentage of overweight, out-of-shape teenagers in the world. Oils, fats, and the meats and cheeses that contain them are linked to high blood pressure, cardiovascular disease, cancers of the colon and breast, and, at latest report, even to loss of eyesight in old age.

Perhaps we value the less nutritious foods because they were once scarce, or "luxuries" only relatively well-to-do people could afford. Maybe it's simply that humans are born with a "sweet tooth" (or a "grease tooth"). For whatever reasons, we don't exactly have the food pyramid upside down, but we certainly have it rearranged. Here's the way it *should not look:*

The Poor Nutrition Pyramid

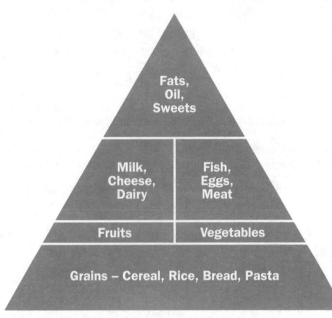

How would your own personal food pyramid look? Is it balanced and healthy, or all out of whack like this one? Do Exercise 2 and find out.

Exercise 2:
Creating Your Personal Food Pyramid

Using the food pyramid on the next page, for the next several days, shade in one small box for each serving of each food you consume in each particular class. (Note that the dairy-eggs-meat and fruits-vegetables parts of the pyramid have been combined to make things simpler.) Be honest in your recording, and don't try to improve your dietary habits until the experiment is over. Just measure the way you actually are eating, right now.

Here are some pointers:

1. Unsweetened fruit juice counts as a fruit serving.

2. Fruit juice or fruit with sugar added counts as a fruit serving, but also counts as one serving under sweets, oils and fats.

3. Two spoonfuls of sugar or a sugar-sweetened soft drink will count as one serving of sweets, oils, and fats.

4. If you eat foods fried in grease or high-cholesterol oil, add a serving to the category of sweets, oils, and fats.

5. If you use salad dressing with sugar in it, score it as a serving of sweets, oils, and fats.

6. Peanut butter goes in the meat-dairy level, but it also scores one for sweets, oils, and fats if it's not a low-cholesterol version.

After a week, or when you have filled all the spaces in any category, the experiment is over. Look at the results and judge for yourself how balanced your diet is and where you need to make adjustments.

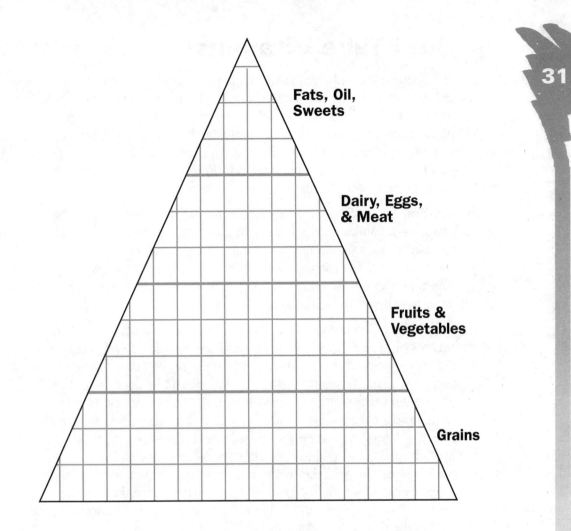

Fats, Oil, Sweets

Dairy, Eggs, & Meat

Fruits & Vegetables

Grains

But I Take Vitamins!

Most people who rationalize an inadequate diet by professing reliance on vitamins are actually saying, "I know I don't eat enough fruits and vegetables, but I get the same nutrients from a vitamin pill." This is only partly true. Certainly, taking a standard daily vitamin supplement is better than taking none at all if you don't get balanced nutrition from what you eat; on the other hand, though, the vitamin matter is somewhat controversial.

Some nutritionists vow that a vitamin from a pill is just as good as one from a natural food source. Others say that certain synthetic laboratory-created vitamins aren't exactly the same as natural ones and don't have the same benefits. All agree on one thing: When you substitute vitamins for fruits and vegetables, you miss out on the other benefits of those foods.

Leafy salads, green and yellow vegetables, and most fruits are also sources of dietary fiber. Low-fiber diets are associated with many digestive system disorders, including cancer of the colon. Also, most people who eat fewer fruits and vegetables usually don't stop there. They often make up the difference with fatty or sweet foods, and some health hazards are associated with a diet too high in fats and sweets—digestive problems and cancers, unstable energy, hypoglycemia, and adult-onset diabetes. Vitamin supplements were made for the purpose the name implies—as supplements. Although it's probably smart to take your vitamins as insurance that you're getting all the vitamins and minerals you need, it's not a good idea to take them as a substitute for healthy eating.

There's some truth in the claims made for "stress vitamins." When you're under stress, you tend to perspire more and to drink more liquids. The result? The water-soluble vitamins wash out of your system more quickly. When you're feeling stressed, then, you probably need a higher vitamin intake, especially of vitamin C and the B-complex vitamins. There are also some good arguments for taking vitamin E, and if you're mentally sluggish, you might increase your choline intake with lecithin. *But it's important not to overdose on vitamins.*

Yes, you can probably overdose on any vitamin. Some are particularly dangerous or bothersome. It's been known for many years, for example, that vitamin A accumulates to toxic levels in the body. Cases of vitamin A poisoning in adults are rare, but they do occur. Recent research has shown a correlation between a daily intake of 10,000+ units of vitamin A by pregnant women and birth defects. These include cleft palate and lip, head abnormalities, and serious heart defects. The damage is done so early in pregnancy that many women aren't even aware they're pregnant yet. This is the first time that excessive intake of a vitamin has proven harmful to the yet unborn. The board of the *New England Journal of Medicine* viewed the findings as so significant that they called a news conference to inform the public before the article even appeared in print.

Side effects from other vitamins are more troublesome than life threatening, so far as we know at this time. But ignoring such an effect is not a good idea. Here are some examples:

- Overdoses of niacin produce an uncomfortable feeling, the "niacin flush." Your face feels hot and may appear reddish, accompanied by a generally "queasy" feeling. Though overuse of niacin is not known to be harmful, no studies exist on long-term overdosage.

- High dosages of vitamin C (ascorbic acid) can result in excess acid in the digestive system and in the urine. Over long periods of time, this could lead to digestive or urinary problems. The sodium ascorbate form of vitamin C may be less likely to produce this kind of problem, but the sodium ion in it may elevate blood pressure, producing another undesirable side effect.

- Some of the B vitamins tend to turn the urine very yellow—a signal that you've reached the dosage of maximum benefit, and further intake will only make it more expensive each time you go to the bathroom.

The bottom line on the vitamins picture? Vitamin supplements are helpful, but should not excuse a tremendously out-of-balance diet. Women of child-bearing age should very carefully monitor their intake of vitamin A (authorities say 5,000 units a day is the maximum safe dose). It may help to take some extra vitamins B, C, and E, and perhaps some lecithin if you are stressed or feeling run down—but don't overdo it. And very importantly, if you detect any vitamin-related discomfort or symptom, reduce your dosage immediately.

But I Need to Lose Weight!

Most people with normal metabolisms don't become overweight if they eat in accordance with the food pyramid principle. Too much fat on the body usually means too many fats and sweets going into the body. The most nutritionally sound way to lose weight is to "chop the top off the pyramid." Eliminate the fats, oils, and sweets from your diet and select only low-fat foods for your quota from the meat and dairy group. Do that, and you'll lose weight gradually and safely.

The problem is, people often get in a hurry, which is why so many have "elevator" weight patterns—up and down. Fad, starvation, or ultra-quick weight-loss regimens trigger the starvation response. When you reach your goal or go off the diet because of frustration, the starvation response tells your body to eat more, and you gain it all back. Another hazard of many diets is that they provide inadequate, unbalanced nutrition or insufficient fiber content. The principles of good nutrition and the food pyramid are especially important during dieting. Again, the answer is to eliminate the "luxury" sweets and fats and choose wisely from the essential categories.

To some people, doing without desserts or fried foods altogether is a very unpleasant prospect, in spite of the need to trim down. There is hope. Here is another simple way to lose weight sensibly:

1. Monitor your food intake and make sure that it's balanced, in proportion to the food pyramid principle.

2. Continue to eat your regular diet, though it occasionally includes steak, fried foods, or chocolate cake—but reduce the portions you eat by a third to a fourth. In other words, eat only two-thirds to three-fourths the *amount* of food in your normal balanced diet pattern. If you would normally have chocolate cake on Sunday, have it, but take a piece only two-thirds the size that you usually would. If you typically have a burger and fries for lunch one day a week, order a smaller size or leave a third to a quarter of each uneaten. There's no law that says you have to "make a happy plate" when your health is concerned.

But I Just Need a Little Boost!

"How long you think that you can run that body down? How many nights you think that you can do what you been doin'?" Yes, there's that song again. The complete line, of course, represents confronting the consequences of another kind of excess that is so much a part of our culture.

We won't take the time or the space here to dwell on the subject of illegal drugs. First of all, they're against the law, and people who use them are subject to imprisonment, fines, and loss of jobs and social standing. Second, there are no quality control standards for drugs sold on the street. It's definitely a "buyer beware" market, and often the awareness of contamination or misrepresentation comes too late. Finally, consumption of illegal drugs exposes you to intentional lawbreakers. And even if the illegally obtained substance is legal when prescribed, the user is taking a potentially dangerous medication without the supervision of a physician. These personal risk factors simply render illegal or illegally obtained drugs out of the question for the intelligent, thinking person.

The comments here will focus instead on the legal and widely used drugs—nicotine, alcohol, and caffeine. There won't be much preaching, just a brief summary of the facts.

Fortunately, smoking and the use of other nicotine delivery systems such as chewing tobacco are rapidly going out of fashion. As a matter of fact, smokers have sort of become dinosaurs in our society—anachronisms, out of step with the times. Those who continue to smoke need only to be reminded that nicotine is a stressor. It constricts the peripheral blood vessels and raises blood pressure. Not only are all kinds of tobacco products carcinogens, smoking adds another stressor. People wouldn't think of inhaling puffs of automobile exhaust. But tobacco smoke contains carbon monoxide just like car exhaust does. The carbon monoxide locks up the red cells in the bloodstream and deprives the body's tissues of oxygen. Most smokers smoke more when heavily stressed. At the time, it creates the illusion of relieving the tension, but it actually adds to the stress and makes the body more susceptible to a stress-related illness.

The same is true of alcohol, when ingested in quantities over about two ounces a day. As you read in Chapter 3, this legal drug has a temporary tranquilizing effect that results in a backlash of increased tension. Drinking more than two cocktails, beers, or glasses of wine a day has a stressful effect on the body. It taxes the liver, interferes with digestion, and irritates the mouth, stomach, and lungs. A hangover is certainly no help when you're already stressed out. Intemperate alcohol consumption also interferes with getting proper rest. It may be hard to stay awake after having "a few too many," but the sleep you get is not the deep, restful kind—it's more like being anesthetized.

Alcohol presents another hazard too. People who use alcohol as a tranquilizer are classifiable as alcohol dependent, meaning they depend on the drug to do something they can't or won't do for themselves. When a person under stress uses alcohol in excessive amounts, that's alcohol abuse—drinking too much. Both are certified diagnoses in the *Diagnostic and Statistical Manual* of the American Psychiatric Association. It's easy to develop a serious alcohol problem by using the chemical in these ways. A person doing so is only one step away from alcohol addiction, another and more severe diagnosis.

If you find yourself drinking more when stressed, and the techniques in this book don't help you stop it, get additional help. Call the nearest office of the National Council on Alcohol and Drug Dependence, the local central office of Alcoholics Anonymous, or a medical professional or treatment center qualified to help you. Alcohol problems are progressive, and you can't predict when they'll worsen. This can happen to anyone. It isn't a matter of character, will power, or moral integrity. It is a medical and psychological problem that needs attention.

The final stressor drug to be discussed here is caffeine, the pick-me-up ingredient in coffee, tea, colas, and other soft drinks. Like alcohol, caffeine in moderation is harmless—it helps you wake up and be more alert, and it may make you feel better. The maximum amount a person can tolerate without the stressor effect varies, depending on how strong the coffee is, the metabolism of the individual, and how habituated to caffeine he or she is. The effect of caffeine seems to be lessened by sugar in the drink, but that creates another negative effect: the possibility of a blood sugar "crash" when the combined effects wear off.

Caffeine increases your blood pressure and heart rate, encourages the elimination of vitamins B and C from your system, irritates your stomach, and may activate your sympathetic nervous system, causing a feeling of panic or "coffee nerves." For most people, the maximum amount is two to four cups of coffee a day, and certainly no more than two or three cups consecutively.

If you suddenly increase the amount of caffeinated beverages you consume, the "coffee nerves" effect will tell you to cut back. If you're a long-term heavy coffee drinker, though, you may not recognize the "caffeine paradox" detected in a study by Dr. Richard Coleman of Stanford University. Coleman found that people who regularly ingested more caffeine than the equivalent of eight to ten cups of coffee a day were actually more sleepy, less alert, and less efficient than if they had consumed none at all. The heavy coffee drinkers tested and performed like people who had been sleep-deprived. They were suffering from caffeine fatigue. Apparently, their bodies had reached the equivalent of GAS phase three: exhaustion. Their long-overtaxed epinephrine-producing systems were no longer able to put out enough of the neurotransmitters to keep them awake and alert.

One of the most graphic studies on the effects of caffeine was performed by pharmacologist Peter Witt and reported in the *Life Nature Library* volume on animal behavior. Witt discovered that when he administered drugs to spiders, their webs showed the impact. Sedatives and tranquilizers caused the spiders to give up or go to sleep before their work was finished. Stimulant drugs caused behavior that might be called "impatient"—the spiders made quick, incomplete, abbreviated webs. The most bizarre effect was caused by caffeine, which resulted in out-of-balance, nonsymmetrical, disorganized patterns.

You might conclude that the moral of this classic experiment is "don't give your spider coffee to drink." Another more relevant conclusion would be "If you don't want your life and work to be jangled and fragmented, limit your intake of caffeine from coffee, tea, chocolate, colas, and other soft drinks."

The Rest of the Story

There's one more part to your basic body fueling and maintenance program for controlling stress: Get enough rest.

A popular comedian once commented: "I sleep like a baby. I wake up cranky every two hours." Worrisome stress can make it difficult to get restful sleep. If this is a problem for you, watch your nutrition and caffeine/alcohol intake, and practice the techniques in this book. If that doesn't help enough, discuss your insomnia with your doctor.

The point is, you can't control stress, perform efficiently, or enjoy life if you're a sleep-deprived zombie. Some people report that they can get by on only a few hours sleep per night. Although it's been proven that certain types of brain injuries seem to wipe out the need for and ability to sleep, this is an exception. Studies have shown that except in rare cases, the people who say they can get by without sleep make up for it by taking naps.

Sleep clinic studies show that humans go through sleep cycles (from light sleep to deep sleep to light again) of approximately ninety minutes each. Most people have to go through five of these cycles in order to awake feeling rested. Because of variations in the length of the cycle and in how long it takes to start to go to sleep, this means the majority of us need approximately seven to eight hours of sleep in order to operate in top condition.

Sleep is not cumulative. You can't "store up extra sleep" to get ready for a series of "short nights." Sleep deprivation, however, is cumulative. You become more stressed and more out of sync with each successive day of too little sleep. The only thing that makes up for lack of sleep is sleeping. Some extra sleep to make up for what was lost is usually necessary, but it's hard to predict exactly how much. In these busy times, it's difficult to guarantee a full night's sleep every night, but you need to get the amount you know you need as often as possible. You also must make up for sleep-deprived nights by taking naps as needed or sleeping longer on weekends.

Sounds fairly simple, right? Eat a nutritious diet based on the food pyramid; use only gradual weight loss programs that keep your diet balanced; avoid or minimize physical stressors like nicotine, alcohol, and caffeine; and get an appropriate amount of rest. There's one more important component of keeping your body in shape for stress control: exercise. That's the subject of the next chapter.

Chapter Five

Stress and Exercise

Although the ancient Greeks were wrong about separating mind from body, they were absolutely correct about the value of physical fitness. (Remember, they were the ones who came up with the Olympics.) There are four good reasons for becoming and staying fit:

1. Fitness gives you the strength and stamina to do the things you want and need to do.

2. Fitness is associated with fewer illnesses and a longer life.

3. Exercise helps relieve and control stress.

4. Exercise can be fun, though not all enjoyable participation sports offer equal stress-control value.

Our earliest ancestors got plenty of exercise just staying alive—obviously it took a great deal of effort to bring game down with primitive weapons, to outrun predators, to migrate many miles on foot, and so on. Even after the discovery of agriculture, work continued by hand along with hunting and herding tasks.

That's the environment in which humans developed. Stress was accompanied by exercise, then followed by relief. Natural systems evolved to release certain hormones and neurotransmitters that mobilized us to act. Then physical exertion released still others to make the stress tolerable. This very old, very basic process is still alive in each of us, but the lower centers of our brains can't distinguish between fear of a sabre-toothed tiger and fear of being fired or not meeting a deadline. The same action response is triggered, and the same chemicals course through our bodies, but the energy has no place to go. We can't run in terror from our place of employment. Physical fighting is inappropriate. We need to do something to use up the fight-flight chemicals and set our bodies in balance again.

Physical exercise is one way to burn off the epinephrine, norepinephrine, and other hormones and neurotransmitters released by stress. Just as the primitive parts of our brains can't tell one kind of fear or anger from another, those same brain structures can't tell the exertion of vigorous exercise from the exertion of combat with a rival or fleeing from a jungle beast.

In addition, regular exercise carries other benefits. It keeps our circulation and muscle tone at a level at which we feel good and are more efficient. It conditions our hearts and lungs for greater strength and resistance to heart attacks. As the blood courses through our veins and arteries, our kidneys and sweat glands get rid of metabolic wastes and other impurities. When we exercise, our bodies even manufacture chemicals that enable us to endure higher levels of stress and have greater tolerance for pain.

As mentioned earlier, the natural body chemicals that increase stress and pain tolerance are called *endorphins*. Endorphin molecules "plug into" receptors in the brain in a way similar to the action of morphine. Morphine is addictive partly because its extended use causes the body to reduce its production of endorphins. When the morphine is gone, the body is without natural or artificial protection from tension and pain.

Vigorous, sustained exercise dramatically increases the production of endorphins. These useful neurotransmitters seem to account in part for the phenomenon of "runner's high," a feeling of well-being and freedom from pain that experienced runners report after a distance of several miles. Endorphin levels not only go up during exercise, but tend to stay higher for hours or even days. If you have ever participated in weight training, you may have noticed that after a week or two you could suddenly lift much heavier weights than before. This is partly because of a gradual increase in strength, but also partly because the exercise increased your endorphin levels and lifting literally didn't hurt as much.

Physical fitness experts advise that any schedule of regular exercise that increases your heart and breathing rates and causes you to work up a sweat will increase your endorphin levels. There's even a widely agreed-upon heart rate formula.

The formula calculates what is approximately 60 percent of your maximum heart rate. Your maximum heart rate is considered to be 220 minus your age. So, if you are forty, your optimal exercise heart rate is 60 percent of (220 - 40), or .60 x 180. That comes out to 108. If you are fifty, it would be 60 percent of (220 - 50), or .6 x 170, which is 102. And so on. Most people don't time their actual heart rate for a full minute. They time it for thirty seconds and multiply by two.

As a matter of fact, most exercisers never time their heart rates or even calculate their optimum exercise heart rate. To get 100 percent maximum cardiovascular benefit from your exercise program, you should do it that way. But if you are getting strenuous enough to feel a little damp with sweat, you're probably exercising in the right range. You do have to keep that pace up for twenty to thirty minutes to get full benefit. (By the way, if your exercise is running and you run for more than thirty minutes, you have surpassed the level of cardiovascular fitness benefit and entered another level, called "training." In other words, you are getting few additional stress control benefits. You are simply learning to run longer, as in training for an event.)

Nobody, not even a professional athlete, should suddenly jump into a new and strenuous sport without being in condition for it. To do so invites strains, sprains, fractures, torn cartlidges, and worse. You don't want reverse results—injury, stroke, or heart attack. Before starting any new exercise program, consult your doctor and make sure you're in good enough shape. Then start at a modest level and gradually work up to full effort over a period of weeks. The guideline for a new exercise program is, "If it seems too easy, you've started at the right level."

Walking? Tennis? Racquetball?

Don't succumb to the tendency to choose a fitness program because it is "in fashion" or because someone else thinks it's the sport for you. Pick something you can enjoy—at least a little. If you really love running, then run. It's a great fitness sport, but unfortunately one in which quite a few injuries occur. If you like the water, join a club with an indoor pool so you can swim all year. If you feel good about yourself when you lift weights, go to a gym. But remember to keep moving. Fitness is about keeping the heart rate up, not about building bulk. Aerobics offer a great workout that can be tailored to various levels of exertion.

One problem with sports like tennis, racquetball, basketball, and softball is that exercise needs to be regular. If you like one of those sports, go for it! But have some alternate activity for days when you don't play. Golf is generally better as recreation than as a fitness sport because it's unlikely to get your heart rate into the optimal range and keep it there. Actually, good, brisk walking for about two miles is one of the best and most natural exercises you can find. Taking a long walk with the dog is just fine if Fido moves at a vigorous pace.

How Often and When?

Most authorities agree that people need some exercise every day. For the cardiovascular type, the generally recommended frequency is at least three or four times a week. In other words, three or four times a week you need to perform some exercise that causes you to "break a sweat" for at least twenty minutes. On the remaining days, do whatever gets you up and moving for a while—one day perhaps a short walk, on another some push-ups and sit-ups, on a third day, a round of golf. The off days are minor or "free choice" exercise days. Most fitness experts agree that participating in very strenuous activity, such as weight lifting with heavy weights, more often than every other day can be counterproductive.

Some people prefer to exercise first thing in the morning to get "up" for the day. Others like to exercise after work to "burn off" tensions. When is best? The answer is simple: Whenever it does you the most good. Usually, that takes into account both your body and your schedule. For example, mornings may be too busy if you have children to get off to school. If you pick a time of day that makes the exercise program add to your stress, that isn't the best time, is it? The most important thing is to DO IT! There are two rules most experts agree on:

1. It's best to exercise before a meal rather than immediately after because the exertion may interfere with digestion.

2. Don't schedule vigorous exercise within an hour or two before bedtime; you're likely to get so perked up that you won't want to sleep.

The following "exercise" exercise can help you make some choices.

Exercise 3:
Choosing Your Exercise Program

Make a list of possible choices for your major cardiovascular fitness exercise program. Remember that you'll need twenty to thirty minutes for each session, and that you'll need to do the exercise three or four times a week. The program does not require the same activity every time. For example, you could swim once a week, walk another day, and play tennis on the third. Write down all the possibilities that come to mind—anything that you think you would like to do and would do.

My Major Fitness Activities

Now that you've listed the major activities you will choose from, use the next section to list the things you might do to get some exercise on the off days. These can be of shorter duration and less strenuous. Again, the idea is to produce a list that you can choose from later.

My "Off-Day" Exercise Activities

_____

_____

_____

_____

_____

_____

_____

_____

_____

_____

_____

_____

Now, use the following calendar (or your own personal calendar/ planner) to schedule your exercise sessions, major and minor, for the next week. Get in the habit of scheduling time to tune up your

Mon.	Tues.	Wed.	Thurs.	Fri.	Sat.	Sun.
Exercise:	Exercise:	Exercise:	Exercise:	Exercise:	Exercise:	Exercise:
Time:	Time:	Time:	Time:	Time:	Time:	Time:
Exercise:	Exercise:	Exercise:	Exercise:	Exercise:	Exercise:	Exercise:
Time:	Time:	Time:	Time:	Time:	Time:	Time:
Exercise:	Exercise:	Exercise:	Exercise:	Exercise:	Exercise:	Exercise:
Time:	Time:	Time:	Time:	Time:	Time:	Time:
Exercise:	Exercise:	Exercise:	Exercise:	Exercise:	Exercise:	Exercise:
Time:	Time:	Time:	Time:	Time:	Time:	Time:

Stress Control

body just like any appointment. An appointment made can always be changed in case of schedule conflict, but appointments never made are seldom kept.

If you find you don't like or have grown tired of a particular activity, choose another from your original list. If the time you chose isn't working out, select another one. Give yourself a pat on the back, and maybe some tangible reward, for keeping your resolve to exercise and stay in shape.

Now that you're on the way to putting your body into maximum shape for stress control, let's turn to the next chapter. We'll move upstairs and start doing something about the mental aspects of stress!

Chapter Six

The Mental Side of Stress

"For there is nothing either good or bad but thinking makes it so." Though many who've seen or read *Hamlet* might consider this comment one of the most memorable lines in the play, few of us probably stop to think how the philosophy applies to us. For example, that most of the harmful stress in our lives exists in our minds.

This is not to say there are no tragedies or catastrophes, actual or potential, in the real world. People must confront wars, street shootings, floods, hurricanes, tornadoes, earthquakes, and a host of other natural and man-made disasters. Our nations and neighborhoods reel from dictators, psychopaths, and child abusers. Someone suffers in the aftermath of drugs, heinous crimes, and deadly epidemics. However, although life does create real victims, few of us have to handle stressors of those proportions—the problem is we *think* as if we did.

Worrying and catastrophizing are among our most formidable enemies. We fear the unlikely and fantasize failure. It's so easy to recognize others overreacting, making mountains out of molehills. But it's often very difficult to have the same insight about ourselves. We are oblivious to the fact that most of our own F-E-A-R is either "false evidence appearing real" or "fantasized evidence appearing real."

Dr. Albert Ellis, creator of rational emotive therapy, points out that most people perceive themselves as victims or potential victims of people and events in the real world. When dissatisfied, worried, fearful, or angry, we are quick to point a finger of blame: "I'm so worried about the downsizing! I'll end up fired!" "It's so stressful and unfair to work for someone who never shows appreciation!" "I have a terrible job! It puts me under pressure twenty-four hours a day!" We see external things—the downsizing, the boss, our jobs—as the cause of distress.

Ellis and others note that our discomfort is actually caused by something else: our beliefs. Most people and events are basically neutral—neither good nor bad, or containing some elements of both. What gets us is our *belief* that the person or event is bad.

The process of resolving difficult emotions by changing our thoughts is called *cognitive therapy*, the therapy of thought. Cognitive therapy frames our discontent in an A-B-C model. "A" is the *activating event* for the process, and the thing we usually blame. For example, my supervisor again failed to say "thank you" when I went the extra mile.

Next comes "B," the (usually unspoken) belief. Sometimes B is a constellation of several *beliefs*. Using the previous example, the beliefs might be "I must even have praise every time I do something right in order to be happy," "It's an awful tragedy when someone fails to give praise," and/or "A person has a right to be and should be miserable when they think they deserve praise and don't get it."

Whatever the belief(s), the process leads to "C," the *consequence*. In the example, it's a dissatisfied state of mind, plus maybe decreased performance on the job if I am dissatisfied enough. Inner consequences lead to outer consequences. For example, if I'm deeply dissatisfied and angry, my behavior, facial expression, and body language change. That, in turn, may lead my boss to back off and become more distant, thus decreasing pleasant interactions (such as praising). The process becomes circular.

Let's look at some other examples of distress as a result of beliefs. Perhaps you are upset because you've been assigned an extra project. The belief involved may be that you can't handle another project, and will fail and be fired. Or, it might be that you believe people should be angry and feel imposed upon if they're assigned more than a certain amount of work, or that you are powerless to assert yourself and turn down an assignment if you become overburdened. You may also believe that you're stuck in your present job and have no choice but to grudgingly do as you are told. Any of these beliefs may be completely true, half true, or totally false, but it's the *belief*, not the project, that causes the distress.

A memo comes out foretelling more planned cutbacks. You feel more stress. Is the cause of the stress the memo? the downsizing? No, those might be listed under "A," the activating event. The cause of the distress lies under "B," the belief. This time, let's burrow even deeper into the belief pattern. First, it would probably be difficult to find anyone who is thrilled with downsizing. To management, it represents a disappointment, perhaps a broken dream regarding the growth of the organization. It also means having to give some good people some rough news. Second, some people will be the recipients of that news—they'll face unemployment. And throughout the ranks of the company, workers will have to adjust to changes in staffing. The employees who are left may see good friends laid off.

No, it's not a cause for celebration. But what about the positive side? The organization will survive, and so will most of the jobs in it. There will be new opportunities with the restructuring. Some of those who are laid off will go on to even greater success and happiness in their new jobs. Some of them didn't like their existing jobs anyway, and would have been better off finding something else years ago. All will survive, and though there may be some period of financial hardship, most will end up in a safer and more realistic financial position. New ways will catch on, more changes will occur, and someday that feared future day of the downsizing will be part of the rosy past.

So, what are these beliefs that make this event result in distress? Here are some possibilities:

1. If the company downsizes, I will be one of those they terminate, and being laid off would be a TRAGEDY because

   A. I would LOSE some possessions I now have.

   B. I will NEVER, ever have another job as good as this one.

   C. My ONLY choice in my job life is to remain in my present job until I am retired or fired.

2. All downsizings are TERRIBLE and UNFAIR because people are RUINED in them. When management lets cutbacks happen, it's because management is STUPID and DOESN'T CARE about people.

3. If the company downsizes, it will be AWFUL because I'll HAVE TO do more work, and

   A. If I am given more to do, I will FAIL and get fired.

   B. When employees are given more to do it is UNFAIR, and management is TAKING ADVANTAGE of us and DOESN'T CARE about us.

   C. I will NEVER get promoted because I am NOT GOOD ENOUGH to compete in a leaner, tougher organization.

Maybe you can come up with still other beliefs that could make the downsizing announcement result in a virtual anxiety attack. Whether you work with the above list or add more, it's pretty easy to see that many of the beliefs have to do with being unimportant, inadequate, powerless, unappreciated, and taken advantage of. The beliefs also often portray others as unconcerned, uncaring, unfair, and opportunistic. The beliefs highlight negative words and phrases, including *tragedy, lose, never, only, terrible, unfair, ruined, stupid, don't care, have to, fail, taking advantage of,* and *not good enough*.

Now, go through that list of beliefs again. This time, put a check mark beside each one that represents your beliefs in case of a similar situation. Do you believe in the "catastrophe" side of the situation, or in the positive side, or both?

Next, go through the beliefs list again and mark each one with a "T" or "F" to note whether, after consideration, you conclude the belief is true or false in the absolute sense. If you sort out your false and questionable beliefs and get rid of that portion of the stress in your life, you will be relieved of quite a load.

Quite simply, what it boils down to is: You can't change "A," the situation. But you can change "B," your beliefs, which in turn changes "C," the consequence.

This I Believe... (Or at Least I Think I Do)

All of us have a basic belief system that we learned from our family or neighborhood culture and from society as a whole. Many of the elements are stereotypes, and many are false or incomplete. However, when you're aware of them, you're free to change them. Sometimes you'll be surprised to find that you also have conflicting beliefs—for example, that real men are sensitive, but real men never cry.

Even if you remain convinced that your basic beliefs are sound, you'll be a more confident person when you become consciously aware of what they are. Along with recognizing positive beliefs, make an earnest effort to include all the negative or conflicting or partially formed beliefs you can think of. Here's an example:

Men...   are stronger than women.

                  don't cry.

                  get taken advantage of by women.

                  must work hard in order to get by.

                  can only get rich if they are dishonest.

The person who would construct a list such as the one above would obviously have many negative beliefs that could lead to distress. Here's another sample list:

Men...   can be sensitive and caring.

                  are equals with women.

                  can enjoy their work if they want to.

                  have many opportunities.

                  don't cry.

This person has many positive beliefs about males, but a major conflicting one too—that men don't cry.

Now, try your hand at the following personal beliefs exercise. Keep your sentences short, and don't try to be tactful or politically correct!

Exercise 4:
Personal Beliefs

1. Men…

_____

_____

2. Women…

_____

_____

3. In our family, men…

_____

_____

4. In our family, women…

_____

_____

5. If I do not meet my goals…

_____

_____

6. When I say what is on my mind…

_____

_____

7. If I were to lose my job…

_____

_____

The Mental Side of Stress

8. Employees usually…

_____

_____

_____

9. Management really…

_____

_____

_____

10. It would be a disgrace if I…

_____

_____

_____

11. People think of me as…

_____

_____

_____

12. Success depends on…

_____

_____

_____

Think over the beliefs you have written down. Discuss them with some people you can be open with. Own them or change them. You may also want to examine your beliefs about specific groups of people, your own assets and weaknesses, or the issue of personal power in general.

You've now taken an important step in looking at beliefs that may or may not lead to distress and "vicious circle" situations. We may not have touched on any areas that are causing you personal stress right now. That comes next. First, a word about false beliefs.

You shouldn't feel shame or guilt about realizing that some of your beliefs are false, questionable, or conflicting. Beliefs are learned, over a period of years, many times. Often, people never even speak them aloud or record them in any way. But they're there just the same. You've formed them even if you haven't actually consciously expressed them. That's why writing them down gives you more insight and confidence. Facing them gives you an opportunity to grow.

Experiments demonstrate that even animals develop "self-fulfilling prophecy" behaviors. In one example, a gerbil is trained to move through a runway to another cage to escape an irritating stimulus, such as a loud noise. Then the "rules" are changed—the horn only sounds if the animal runs at least halfway down the runway, though the noise still stops when the little guy gets to the second cage. The gerbil will continue to run for the rest of its life to *get* the very thing it's trying to get away from. You might say the gerbil "thinks" it has to run or something frightening will happen. Unfortunately, you can't pick the little fellow up and explain that the rules have changed, or that there is new evidence. Fortunately, humans are verbal—by talking things out and writing things down, we can escape from our self-defeating beliefs.

Now look at a stressful circumstance in your life and apply the A-B-C model to find at least one false belief associated with the situation. (There's bound to be at least one.) In Exercise 5, use the A-B-C method (activating event-belief-consequence) to analyze the beliefs behind one major cause of distress you identify in your life.

Exercise 5:
The A-B-Cs of One of My Stressors

A. The actual event–superficial (not real) cause of the distress

I associate this stress in my life with this situation, event, or person and behavior:

_____

_____

_____

_____

_____

_____

B. The belief system–the (real) cause of the distress

I believe the way things should be is... (If you're filling in this section correctly, each negative belief will contain a major negative phrase like *can't, don't, have to, fail, failure, should, shouldn't, never, only, tragedy, catastrophe, terrible, stupid, don't care, taking advantage of, ruined, lose, unfair,* or *not good enough.*)

_____

_____

_____

_____

_____

_____

C. The consequences of the event as filtered through the belief

The outcome of passing this event or situation through the filter of my beliefs is...(Examples are "I feel stressed," "I get angry," or "I behave _____ and that makes the situation worse because..."

_____

_____

_____

_____

_____

_____

A large number of widely respected authorities—including Albert Ellis, Maxie Maultsby, Wayne Dyer, Will Schutz, Aaron Beck, and David Burns—emphasize using the process you have just experienced in order to become a more DIStress-free person. Finding and doing something about your false "catastrophizing" beliefs will make you a happier person. If you want to explore the healing power of the thought process in greater detail, you may want to read some of the books listed in the Bibliography and Suggested Reading list at the end of this book.

Roadblocks to New Beliefs

Though you may have misgivings or feel uneasy about giving up old beliefs, realize (and take strength from the fact) that you have the power of choice. *You* control the shift in thinking. Richard Bandler and John Grinder make the point that our belief system is like a map that exists in our minds. The map is not the territory. To paraphrase their commentary on the uncertainty of many of our beliefs, "Most of your own reality is made up, so if it's making you unhappy, why not make up a new reality that serves you better?"

Another problem some of us have when it comes to changing our beliefs and behaviors is guilt. "If I admit I was wrong, I have to feel guilty." (Does that sound like a negative belief?) Guilt has some value. It's good long enough to get us to change our ways, and to say "I'm sorry" if that's called for. Beyond that, though, guilt is useless. Do you feel guilty that you soiled your diapers when you were a baby? Of course not. That was the best you could do at the time, and you wouldn't intentionally do so now. Most of our self-defeating or incorrect beliefs and behaviors are like that. They were the best we could do at the time. Like the gerbil in the experiment, we just didn't realize the real rules of the game. Give yourself a "guilt-ectomy." Take the no-guilt pledge:

Once I have corrected an incorrect thought or behavior, and have stopped thinking or behaving that way, and have apologized to anyone who deserves an apology, I promise to recognize that my temporary guilt has served me well and I will feel guilty no more.

Exercise 6 builds on the previous one you completed, Exercise 5, "The A-B-Cs of One of My Stressors." Make a number of copies of the Stressor Reevaluation Form, and use one to evaluate each major stressful person, thing, or event in your life. As you do, remember the choice principle:

I GET WHAT I TAKE,

I TAKE WHAT I WANT,

AND I PAY FOR IT ALL.

If you have some trouble accepting that statement, think of it this way: If you have success in this world, you may say it's because "I actively take that success for myself." On the other hand, if you put up with a lot of really unfair treatment, you may say, "I take a lot of punishment." (Here "take" is used in the passive sense.) I get what I take. All right, you say, but are you telling me someone wants the unfair treatment? Yes, in the sense that it's a "bottom line" statement. Everything has its price. The price of getting away from that punishing environment probably means taking a risk—looking for a new job, facing possible rejection, terminating a relationship, being alone, taking the chance that your new situation may be no better than the one you are leaving. If you decide that the price of getting away is too high, you remain in the unfair situation out of *choice*. At the bottom line, you determine the result: You take what you want from what you see as the available choices.

Exercise 6:
Stressor Reevaluation Form

A. The stressor, the superficial cause of my stress is:

_____

_____

_____

_____

B. The belief that causes me to experience this as DIStressful is:

_____

_____

_____

_____

C. The consequences, my feelings, and my counterproductive behaviors, are:

_____

_____

_____

_____

Reevaluation

1. The reason or belief that causes me to stay in this situation is:

_____

_____

_____

_____

2. After thinking about all of this and talking it over with someone, I have decided that belief is... *(Check one)*

_____True and valid.

_____False or incomplete.

3. After thinking about all of this and talking it over with someone, I have decided that my reason for enduring the stressor in A is... *(Check one)*

_____True and valid.

_____False or incomplete.

4. Some changes in my beliefs, actions, or behaviors that could eliminate this DIStress are...

_____

_____

_____

_____

_____

_____

_____

5. After considering my options, I have chosen to do the following: *(Check one)*

_____Remain in the situation and change nothing.

_____Get out of the situation involving the stressor.

_____Change my belief about the situation.

_____Change a behavior.

The Mental Side of Stress

6. Unless you've chosen to remain in the situation and change nothing, explain your choice briefly. If you're getting out of the situation, what is your plan? If you're changing something about yourself, what is that belief or behavior?

_____

_____

_____

_____

_____

_____

_____

_____

_____

Now you've identified the basics of beating the mental side of stress: Locate your false beliefs, discover positive realities, use guilt appropriately and then let go of it, and continue to reevaluate your stress producers. The next chapter will take your mind-power a step further in controlling stress and changing your life for the better.

Chapter Seven

Positive Results

With all those mental habits that add up to DIStress, it's obvious we need to do what the old song says: "Accentuate the positive, eliminate the negative." We need some positive results!

"Yes," someone else replies, "all those negative people make me so *mad!*"

Ah! There's the "Catch-22." The irony of getting angry about negativity is striking. Anger, itself, is classified as a "negative" emotion, and one we don't want to feel any more often than absolutely necessary. Anger is the "fight" part of the fight-or-flight syndrome. And here we are experiencing a negative emotion because we object to someone else's negativity. That irony should awaken you to just how contagious negativity and DIStress can be.

Not only do the protestations of your discontent echo in the unfulfilled spaces of your own life—they're also capable of producing an equal (and not opposite) reaction in someone else. The distressed around us argue for us to join them in their misery. If they sell us on the correctness of their unhappiness, we've fallen into DIStress. If we become too upset about our difference of perspective, we've again lapsed into DIStress. Between the two extremes is the balance beam of tranquillity that seems so hard to walk.

Here we can join author-counselor John Bradshaw in borrowing some wisdom from twelve-step programs. And why not? Since the 1930s, these programs have been helping people solve some of the most serious stress-related problems—alcoholism, drug addiction, eating disorders, co-dependency, and compulsive gambling, to name a few. If the twelve-step ideas can help people with problems like those, maybe those of us with lesser problems should give some of the principles a try.

The Secret to Peace of Mind

One of these principles is acceptance, the secret to peace of mind in an often troubled world. The anonymous author of an essay in a major twelve-step program textbook encapsulates the idea brilliantly:

"And acceptance is the answer to ALL my problems today. When I am disturbed, it is because I find some person, place, thing, or situation—some fact of my life—unacceptable to me, and I can find no serenity until I accept that person, place, thing, or situation as being exactly the way it is supposed to be at this moment."

The writer goes on to say that we often need to focus not so much on what needs to be changed in the world as on what needs to be changed in ourselves and our attitudes.

Some people reject this philosophy immediately because they misunderstand it. They protest, "But if I accept everything as it is, that means I have to accept war, crime, and injustice in society! It means I have to accept my salary as OK, and I want more! It means I have to accept my supervisor's uncaring attitude, and I don't like it! Those things are UNacceptable!"

The person who rails so hard against this principle as the key to defeating DIStress has missed two important phrases in the message of acceptance. The first is "at this moment." If there's a war going on, or crime in the streets, or social injustice in our communities, those things are realities. They are not going to go away in the next five minutes, or perhaps ever, completely. The people causing those situations are, unfortunately, doing what seems natural to them. You might say they're doing the best they can, based on who they are (out of their own experiences). Much the same may be said about salaries and supervisors—there is no magic wand to wave and make them change immediately. When we become angry, fearful, distressed over these facts of life, our energy is consumed by emotion. Our clear thinking turns to doomsaying, daydreaming, or thoughts of revenge. The power to actually *do* anything about the situation escapes us.

The second phrase that qualifies the acceptance message is "not so much." The writer did not say that we should never try to change anything in the world around us. He or she does not imply that we should never dedicate ourselves to causes. Acceptance does not mean no chance for change. As a matter of fact, it means new energy to encourage change and more incisive, logical thinking to steer that course. In some cases, acceptance is perhaps the only chance for change.

One example is the case where we become distressed about other people's behavior and embark on a crusade to change it. A man walking down the street happened to see a little boy in his front yard pulling a cat's tail. The cat was making quite a ruckus, and the passerby thought the boy needed a lesson in kindness to animals. "Little boy, stop pulling that cat's tail!" instructed the man. The boy replied, "I'm not pulling the cat's tail." "Yes, you are," the adult responded. "I can see with my own two eyes that you have the cat's tail in your hand and you are pulling it very hard." "Oh, no," said the boy. "I'm just holding on. The cat's doing all the pulling." Recognizing that there's another point of view is a crucial step in acceptance. And sometimes, if the situation is going to change, there has to be some "letting go."

The anonymous author of the wise tidbit about acceptance had another thing right: Acceptance starts with change inside you. That's what sometimes makes it so hard to master the acceptance habit. But like all habits, though difficult to start, acceptance becomes ingrained, flowing more easily as time goes along. It simply becomes a part of your natural way of dealing with the world.

The road to acceptance begins the journey toward more power and peace of mind. To boost yourself along, complete Exercise 7.

Exercise 7:
What I Am Having a Hard Time Accepting

A. First, list several things you have a hard time accepting. If your list won't fit in the space provided, get some more paper. Make it a very personal list of hard-to-accept realities in your daily life that cause you anger or fear, such as "My spouse is too moody and doesn't give me enough closeness" or "I have to work overtime, and I don't like giving up my time off." In other words, leave worldwide or community issues for later.

_____

_____

_____

_____

_____

_____

_____

_____

_____

_____

_____

_____

Positive Results

B. Hard to swallow as they may be, each item on that list is a fact of your life. In keeping with the principle of acceptance, you next need to go back to each item and ask yourself this question: "What could I change about myself or my attitude that would make that person or situation more bearable?" Here are some examples of how this works:

Fact of Life

- My supervisor seems uncaring and doesn't give me enough praise.

Things I Could Change

- Realize it's HIS problem.

- Give myself the praise I need.

- Make up for the cold atmosphere by associating with appreciative people.

- Do such a good job I can't be ignored.

- Look for a job working for someone who gives praise.

Fact of Life

- My salary is too low, and I have a hard time living on it.

Things I Could Change

- Be more practical. Live on a budget.

- Get a second, "moonlighting" job.

- Get some more training and prepare for a promotion.

- Ask for extra projects or overtime to earn more money.

Fact of Life

- My spouse is too moody and doesn't give me enough closeness.

Things I Could Change

- Realize it's not my responsibility to make another person happy.

- Be more considerate and appreciative to encourage more closeness.

- Express myself more intimately to open the channel of communication.

- Give my partner some "space" until he or she is ready to communicate.

- Become less dependent, make more friends, be less needy.

- Leave the relationship.

Now it's your turn.

Fact of Life _____

_____

_____

Things I Could Change _____

_____

_____

_____

_____

_____

Fact of Life _____

_____

_____

Things I Could Change _____

_____

_____

_____

_____

Fact of Life _____

_____

_____

Things I Could Change _____

_____

_____

_____

_____

Fact of Life _____

_____

_____

Things I Could Change _____

_____

_____

_____

_____

Staying Tuned to the Right Station

Once established, the acceptance habit will keep you happy every moment for the rest of your life, right? Wrong. First of all, legitimately sad and disappointing situations come along every now and then, and some of them are significant enough that it takes a while to accept them. Second, there are times when you're cruising along with your mental radio tuned to the positive and accepting station and then, without warning, a negative thought interferes.

There are two reasons the radio analogy works well when it comes to the intrusion of negative thoughts. First, with a car radio, there's some reason in the real world that interference breaks in. Maybe you didn't have the receiver tuned precisely. Maybe you were traveling in territory where the signal was wearing thin. Or perhaps some other reality, such as a sudden rainstorm, changed what your receiver was picking up. The same is true in listening to your "peace of mind" program—you can get a little off the beam, stray too far from the source, or receive a random "signal" or message from the environment.

The second reason the radio analogy is effective is that often that negative signal takes the form of "words heard in our mind." Sometimes it's more like television—accompanied by a picture. But always the negative message is followed by a feeling of distress.

Hundreds, maybe thousands of times a day, we talk to ourselves without speaking aloud. Most of these inner conversations are useful, but some are irrelevant or strangely placed. In the middle of an important business presentation, the voice in your head asks if your hair looks all right, or wonders if you're supposed to stop at the store on the way home. Many inner verbalizations are automatic—you see or experience a particular thing and automatically think a standard thought. It's the inner version of the old classroom automatic response. The teacher calls your name, and you say "here." Distressful inner speech also is often automatic. If you haven't had a certain distressful thought for some time, it's because you haven't experienced the stimulus it goes with.

Those inner conversations of ours can be fascinating. There are many voices, representing the many different roles we play and have played, and coming from many different times in our lives. There are other people's voices too—your mother's, your dad's, a former school teacher's, and on and on. Each of us, for each issue we consider, has an inside-the-head committee trying to influence us. And not every voice on the committee is positive and accepting.

When you hear that negative signal jamming your peaceful channel, you need to practice what psychologists call "thought stopping." Simply recognize that an intruding thought is damaging your peace of mind and say, "Stop!" Say it out loud or silently; either way, it's an excellent device.

Some people note a tendency to say, "Stop, stupid!" (Nice way to treat yourself, right?) That's not the correct way to practice thought stopping. When "stupid" or other derogatory words pop in almost automatically, though, it may give you pause to wonder whose voice from the committee is coming through. The idea is to stop the thought and take control of your thoughts, not to belittle or punish yourself. Self-esteem author Jack Canfield uses the word "cancel" instead of "stop," possibly because "cancel" is less likely to be followed by some internal put-down.

There is one problem with thought stopping as a cure-all for distressful thinking. To experience it, follow these directions. First, think of a giraffe. Close your eyes for a few seconds and think intently about that giraffe—winsome faced, long necked, bony kneed. Now lay the book aside and stop thinking about the giraffe for one minute. During that minute, do not think about a giraffe. Under no circumstances are you to think of a giraffe for a full minute.

Didn't work, did it? It's difficult, if not impossible, to stop a thought by using the intention to stop it. Somehow, our very resolve to stop seems to call attention to the thing we want to quit doing. At best, it's like telling someone to stop doing something incorrectly without showing them what is correct. The best way to stop a distressing thought is to replace it with something that is not distressing.

For some people, dwelling on a meditative phrase is all it takes to turn distressful, counterproductive thinking around. Others prefer alternatives that involve doing positive things and putting themselves in contact with positive people. Examples are reading something uplifting, doing a favor or service for someone, seeking out something of beauty such as music or art, or calling some positive-minded, nondistressful friend. (Negative people are poison to peace of mind. As one humorist put it, "If you hang out with ducks all the time, eventually you'll quack.")

Exercise 8:
My Strategies to Replace Distressful Thoughts

What will you do to replace distressful thoughts when they intrude, as intrude they will? Use the space below to write down at least three possibilities. Be specific. For example, if one strategy is to call a friend, list the names of at least three positive-minded, nourishing friends you could call.

_____

_____

_____

_____

_____

_____

_____

_____

_____

_____

_____

_____

_____

_____

_____

_____

An Ounce of Prevention

Since calming, accepting thoughts can successfully replace distressful negative ones, wouldn't it be wonderful if there was something you could do to minimize the number of negative thoughts you have? Wouldn't it be great if you could influence your life so that there'd be fewer distressful happenings and more successes? The good news is, there *is* a way!

You can store up positive, calm, successful thoughts and images through the power of positive visualization. By visualizing a positive future, one in which both you and the world have changed for the better, you can make the past and present feel much more acceptable. Though few people take the time to do it, this is an important process. Do you remember the childhood game called "What's Missing in This Picture?" The human mind is like that. Without goals and a vision of the future, we tend to focus on what's missing in our present picture of the world.

To start the process of believing in your future, complete Exercise 9.

Exercise 9:
Setting My Goals

A. Write down five to ten goals you'd like to accomplish in the next five or so years. They don't even have to be what most people would call "realistic," though it would be fruitless to choose goals no human being could accomplish. Fill the list with things you really want (go back to college and graduate, travel to Africa, become manager of a major company, appear on network television, write a best-selling book, take guitar lessons from Eric Clapton, etc.).

My Goals: I Want To...

_____

_____

_____

_____

_____

_____

_____

_____

B. Now that you have your list of goals, think each one through clearly. Use the next several pages to write some notes on the details of each. If you wanted to get a degree, what does it look like? Will you get a class ring? Where will you hang your diploma? What will your office or work area look like when you achieve your goal? What will *you* look like? And so on. Get ready with all the details of how the situation will look when you have successfully accomplished your goal and how it will look and feel to be you, experiencing and being a part of that.

When you've completed your notes, take at least fifteen minutes to visualize the complete picture. Make a movie in your mind that shows you successfully accomplishing your goals. Sometimes the "camera" will be showing you; sometimes it will be seeing things from your perspective. Notice that you feel relaxed and DIStress-free in your visualization.

When you've completed your visualization, you will have internalized your goals and set your subconscious mind to notice the opportunities to accomplish them. If you particularly like the visualization process, do it again in a day or two. Most authorities agree that the more frequently you visualize, the better it works and the more and more likely you are to accomplish your goals sooner and more easily. Before you read on, stop and do a visualization of your future calm, serene, successful life.

Goal #1:

_____

_____

_____

_____

_____

_____

_____

_____

_____

Goal #2:

_____

_____

_____

_____

_____

_____

_____

_____

_____

Goal #3:

_____

_____

_____

_____

_____

_____

_____

_____

_____

Goal #4:

_____

_____

_____

_____

_____

_____

_____

_____

_____

_____

_____

Goal #5:

_____

_____

_____

_____

_____

_____

_____

_____

_____

Goal #6:

_____

_____

_____

_____

_____

_____

_____

_____

_____

_____

Goal #7:

_____

_____

_____

_____

_____

_____

_____

_____

_____

Goal #8:

_____

_____

_____

_____

_____

_____

_____

_____

_____

Goal #9:

_____

_____

_____

_____

_____

_____

_____

_____

_____

Goal #10:

_____

_____

_____

_____

_____

_____

_____

_____

_____

_____

_____

Half Empty or Half Full?

Goals can take a while to accomplish. Some come more quickly than expected, some more slowly. The unconscious process that seeks and finds opportunities to reach goals is not a good judge of the passage of time. But what if there were something you could do *now* to relieve DIStress resulting from the "what's missing in this picture" tendency we all have? Something that could relieve the DIStress *before* you accomplish your goals? There is—it's called a gratitude list.

A gratitude list is simply a list of all the things in your life that you're grateful for, such as your health, your friends and family, your skills and unique attributes, and so on. So often we become obsessed with the idea that our "cup is half empty" that we forget that by definition it's also half full!

Use Exercise 10 to start creating your gratitude list.

Exercise 10:
My Gratitude List

Use the space below to compile a list of things you're grateful for.
Include all the things that in your most joyful moments you want to
shout "Thank you!" for.

_____

_____

_____

_____

_____

_____

_____

_____

_____

_____

_____

_____

_____

_____

_____

_____

_____

_____

For most people, completing a list such as the one you wrote in Exercise 10 is one of the most freeing of experiences. For all of our wants and our goals, it's also reassuring to acknowledge the things we already have that make life worth living.

One item that most people include on their gratitude lists is their job or something about their job. However, work-related items on heartfelt gratitude lists tend to be overwhelmingly outnumbered by things not related to job and career. Use Exercise 11 to write another gratitude list—this one strictly related to your life at work. Call it "Positives About My Job."

Exercise 11:
Positives About My Job

List all the things you're grateful for about your job. Here are some examples:

- I like the people I work with.

- I am glad I work at something I basically enjoy.

- My present job is preparing me for the one I have always wanted to do.

- I'm glad I get to work with people.

- I enjoy working outdoors.

- Our company has fair policies and a good benefits plan.

_____

_____

_____

_____

_____

_____

_____

_____

_____

_____

_____

_____

The number of positives people can list about their jobs vary widely. Some can write several pages. Some can come up with only eight or ten. If you could not think of at least five positives about the job you now hold (including future opportunities and the people you work with), it may be time to think about relocating.

Most people who do Exercise 11 are impressed by the fact that their pleasant or joyful feelings aren't as strong for most of the items on their job gratitude list as they were on their life gratitude list. That's to be expected. Not many people find the closeness in relationships on the job that they do with family and close friends. Few feel as grateful for even a very high salary as they do for good health, a clear mind, and a good sense of values. The point is, there are positives in all areas of our lives, and you'll feel less DIStress when you focus on them. Just don't forget which list is more important.

Now with new energy and acceptance, and a better perspective on your life and where you're headed, let's move on to another important aspect of stress control—being assertive.

Chapter Eight

Stress and Assertiveness

By now, if you've done all the exercises, you've learned to reevaluate your beliefs and let go of those that are false. You've also had the opportunity to examine the people and situations in your life that you find hard to accept and to consider what you would have to change about yourself to accept them. You probably decided that some things were best accepted and left alone. But with others, although you now see the wisdom of accepting the situation for the time being, you still have hopes of seeing things change in the future. That's where assertiveness comes in.

If your understanding of assertiveness is like that of most people, you associate asserting yourself with asking for what you want and saying "no" when someone makes an unrealistic request. These are two elements of assertiveness, but by no means the complete picture.

When assertiveness training became accepted in the 1970s, it was because of books like *When I Say No I Feel Guilty* by Manuel Smith and the first edition of *Your Perfect Right* by Robert Alberti and Michael Emmons. These helping professionals had noticed large numbers of people who were distressed because they found it hard to stand up for themselves. The authors all made the point that assertiveness is not being "pushy." They all agreed that assertive communication is the rational midground between passive "doormat" behavior and "steamroller" aggressiveness. They defined assertiveness as communicating as an equal, a win-win kind of position. But after a decade or more of assertiveness training, the general public seemed to identify assertiveness with being aggressive, or at least demanding and uncooperative.

There were reasons for this misconception. One was the faulty training of well-meaning teachers who hadn't bothered to study the matter in depth and become fully qualified. But a major explanation rested in the people who sought the assertiveness training or read the books. For the most part, they were people who weren't very communicative to begin with. After some exposure to the idea of assertiveness, they began to communicate their wants and to say "no," but their communication did not increase (improve) in other areas.

This has prompted some of the founders of the assertiveness movement to produce a new and clearer definition of being assertive, as is found in the latest edition of *Your Perfect Right*. Two ideas that were present in the original philosophy but that weren't emphasized very strongly come through loud and clear now: One is that assertiveness means expressing yourself in *all* things— expressing liking, loving, and appreciation as well as those things we don't appreciate. The other idea is that we need to assert ourselves *with ourselves* as well as with other people.

Being Assertive With Yourself

Begin by asserting yourself in positive ways. Use Exercise 12 to list at least ten things you appreciate and like about yourself. If you can list forty or fifty, that's even better! It's not the same thing as bragging; you don't have to feel guilty about appreciating the positive things about you. You don't even have to lose your humility. After all, there are many people who have the same good qualities or the same number of other qualities.

Exercise 12:
Things I Appreciate About Myself

Write down at least ten things you like about yourself. If you can think of more than that, go ahead and list them. As you write each positive statement, say to yourself, "I appreciate me for that."

_____

_____

_____

_____

_____

_____

_____

_____

_____

_____

_____

_____

_____

_____

_____

_____

_____

_____

_____

Asserting Yourself Positively With Others

Listing the things you appreciate about yourself may have been difficult, but it was good practice for what comes next—asserting yourself positively with others around you. Even though we're usually better about complimenting others and telling them positive things, we still take others for granted at times, or feel too busy or embarrassed to express appreciation. In Exercise 13, list the people you need to express acceptance, appreciation, approval, love, or other positive feelings to.

When you stay on top of these appreciative assertions you're much more likely to be successful when you start asking for the things you want. Others will recognize you as a warm, well-rounded, complete human being they enjoy and appreciate. Expressing appreciative assertions is your guard against being seen as pushy, aggressive, or uncooperative when your wants or needs aren't the same as those of others.

Exercise 13:
Asserting Myself Positively With Others

In the space provided below, list the names of the people you need to assert yourself positively to, what it is you need to express, and when you intend to assert your positive feeling. Here are some examples:

Person	I need to assert...	Date
My husband	"I love you."	As soon as I see him this afternoon.
Mary	Appreciation for ten years of friendship.	When I see her Monday.
My daughter	Approval of the way she has improved her grades.	Write her a letter at college, tonight.
My supervisor	"I like working for you."	Next time she pays me a compliment.

Person _____

I need to assert... _____

_____ **Date** _____

Person _____

I need to assert... _____

_____ **Date** _____

Person _____

I need to assert... _____

_____ **Date** _____

Telling Yourself What You Want

Before you can tell others what you want, you must know what you want from them—and be comfortable with wanting it. As with the loving variety, the best place to start with the "I want" type of assertion is with yourself. In other words, practice "I want" assertions by being assertive with yourself, by getting firm with yourself about really taking the steps toward doing something you've been putting off, such as cleaning the garage. Or maybe there's something you've been wanting to change about yourself, such as to stop saying "yes" when you need to say "no." To be properly assertive, avoid the words "should" or "shouldn't" as well as words and phrases that imply a put-down, such as "stupid," "lazy," and "no excuse." For example, say "I will clean the garage on Saturday," not "I should stop being lazy and clean the garage." You can practice being properly assertive with yourself in Exercise 14.

Exercise 14:
Things I Want From Me

List at least two or three things that you want to do but have been putting off, or things you've wanted to change about yourself for some time (clean the basement, enroll in a continuing education class, take a real vacation, stop saying "yes" when you need to say "no," etc.).

Then go back and add the date when you want to start each thing on your list. Stick to it. Remind yourself of your start date, and do it.

Things I Want   **Start Date**

_____   _____

_____   _____

_____   _____

_____   _____

_____   _____

_____   _____

_____   _____

_____   _____

_____   _____

_____   _____

_____   _____

_____   _____

Being Assertive With Others

By practicing being assertive on yourself, you'll be better prepared for what most people have in mind when they start working on assertiveness—asking others for things you want. This part of asserting yourself adds more wisdom to the motto in Chapter 6 ("I get what I take, I take what I want, and I pay for it all"). A successful sales manager used to give his staff this bit of advice about asking directly for the order: "My grandmother used to tell me, 'If you don't ask...you don't get.'"

Asking is very important. Assertion is communicating as an equal—calmly, adult to adult, requesting or negotiating things you deserve. It's part of what Virginia Satir was talking about when she described "levelling"—straight-on, nonblaming, nonapologizing communication.

Asserting involves "I" statements and "we" statements rather than blaming statements using the word "you." Asserting means becoming calm and feeling equal yourself so that your pace, vocal inflection, facial expression, and body language match the logical tone of your request. Assertion is taking responsibility for your own wants, needs, and feelings. It often means being willing to negotiate, compromise, or offer something in return for what you want. It has nothing to do with "getting somebody told" or "getting even."

With that in mind, complete Exercise 15. In this exercise, limit yourself to three people or issues you want to start asserting yourself about. If better assertion is a goal for you, your actual list is probably much longer, but it's best to work on one person or issue at time. Long lists tend to become "complaint lists" that help you identify as a victim, feel overwhelmed, and take no specific action. Short, specific lists get positive, time-specific results.

As you begin asserting yourself with one specific person or on one particular issue, add another person or issue to your list. But don't forget to continue being assertive with the earlier people or issues as you add to your list.

Soon you'll find that assertiveness has become a habit. As wonderfully effective as it can be, though, assertiveness is not a magical process that guarantees you'll always get what you want when you want it. In that sense, success takes patience and flexibility. Life is a continuing process of reevaluating your beliefs to decide whether they are false or unrealistic, searching your soul to determine what you need to accept as is, and where you need to apply your energy to encourage change in your life. You have the right to say "no," and so do other people. You have the right to ask, and so do they. Compromise is always a gain, never a defeat.

Exercise 15:
Asserting Myself With Others

Make a list of what you want from others that you need to be assertive about. State when you will begin to assert yourself with this person. (In some cases, it may not be a specific person, but rather a group or a class of people with whom you haven't been assertive on a particular issue.) Here are some examples:

Person	I need to assert...	Date
My supervisor	Ask for a recommendation for promotion	Next personnel review, August
My children	Ask for them to do their chores without complaining	After school today
My co-workers	The right to say "no" when they ask for help and I'm too busy	The next time one asks and I'm already overloaded

Now you try.

Person _____

I need to assert... _____

_____ **Date**_____

Person _____

I need to assert... _____

_____ **Date**_____

Person _____

I need to assert... _____

_____ **Date**_____

Stress and Assertiveness

Sometimes, too, you ask the wrong person, someone without the power to grant your request—or the courage. Sometimes your wants may involve someone who is dishonest, corrupt, addicted, abusive, thoroughly self-centered, or otherwise not whole emotionally, morally, or spiritually. When you find yourself asking for something you truly need from someone who isn't capable of giving it, there are only two possible choices: give up the goal, or disengage from that person and seek your goal elsewhere.

When you're having trouble making up your mind about a situation, it helps to get some distance. Try the following visualization exercise on some situation that is distressful to you.

Exercise 16:
Taking Flight

Sit in a comfortable place, close your eyes, and pretend you're dreaming or in a trance. In your imagination, feel and see your consciousness leave your body and float up to the ceiling, above yourself. From there, you can look down and see yourself sitting with your eyes closed. Since it's only your consciousness that's floating up and your body will stay in the chair, you're perfectly safe and have no need to fear the height.

Since because your floating consciousness has no density, it can pass right up through the ceiling and on outdoors. Your consciousness has the gift of seeing right through walls and buildings and other barriers. You can transcend time. You can float up to just the right height, and look down on yourself with the person or situation that's distressing you at a time when the problem is actually happening. Let your consciousness float around there and observe what's going on for a while. There's no hurry.

Now allow your consciousness to float higher, until you can see an entire section of town, and can look into all the houses and buildings and see all the various things people are doing there. Float higher until you can see your whole city, your whole state, or the entire region. You may decide to let your consciousness gradually float higher until you can see the Earth turning beneath you, and all the continents and people of the world.

Now begin a gradual, leisurely descent. Your consciousness comes floating back down, floating over the problem situation again for another glimpse, perhaps a little more insight and then back to the room where your consciousness will rejoin your body. When you have come back down and feel centered in yourself, open your eyes.

Stress and Assertiveness

Many people who practice the visualization in Exercise 16 report that it helps them notice things they weren't aware of when they were "too close to the situation." They also report that it helps them put the issue involved in better perspective. Visualization is also very good practice for some of the major stress relief techniques that you will learn and practice in the next chapter.

Chapter Nine

Major Relaxation Techniques

In Chapter 1, you learned some techniques for quickly relieving the immediate tensions of stress. Many stress management programs would have moved immediately from those brief exercises to the deep relaxation techniques that are the major stress relievers.

The present approach saves them for now because, though the techniques have some protective value against stress, they are primarily for breaking the tension of already existing stress symptoms. In the long run, you're better off doing something about the physical and emotional causes of unnecessary distress, and then learning how to become even more effective in the face of the normal and unavoidable stressors of living.

The major relaxation techniques that you'll explore here provide a chance to rest and recharge your batteries.

During and after relaxation, blood pressure and heart rate are lower. Breathing is deeper and more regular. About twenty minutes in a deeply relaxed state makes a profound difference in how you feel. Most of the techniques used to produce this relaxation also have a paradoxical effect. They can be used to refresh you mentally and physically so you can be more alert, but they can also be used to prepare you for restful sleep. Whether the result is alert or asleep depends on your mind-set when you begin the relaxation—with one exception. If you're fatigued and sleep deprived, you may fall asleep during the relaxation, regardless of your intentions.

The techniques that are most frequently used to produce the tranquil, healing state are *progressive relaxation* and *relaxation imagery*. Other meditative practices, including yoga, gentle body realignment exercises, massage, and various forms of meditation can produce the same result. If you already know one of these disciplines and like its effect, practice it twenty minutes a day. It will make a big difference.

If you don't know any techniques yet, it's easy to learn them. Like many practices that relieve the effects of stress, there doesn't seem to be any "most correct" way to do any of them. Whatever works for you is fine, and you'll get better and better with more practice.

Progressive Relaxation

Some people find it very difficult to relax when they want to. Progressive relaxation simplifies the process by letting you relax your body one section at a time. It also makes it easier by helping you remember how it feels to relax and let tension go. This is done by consciously tensing all the muscles in a particular area of the body and then relaxing that area. You begin at your head or your feet and gradually progress to the other end of your body. Most people can do a good job of performing progressive relaxation after just reading the following directions; however, if it's hard for you to do it that way, ask someone to read you the instructions a couple of times while you practice. Here's the step-by-step process, starting from your head and working down:

1. Lie down in a comfortable position, on your back, and close your eyes. It's best not to cross your arms or legs or clasp your hands together. Get into a position that will remain comfortable if you are motionless for twenty minutes or so.

2. Breathe easily and deeply for a minute or so, concentrating on breathing with your abdomen—not by puffing up your chest when you inhale. Allow whatever relaxation that comes to happen.

3. Pay attention to your head and face. Make all the muscles there tense. Squeeze your eyes tightly shut, press your lips together, and make an ugly face. Then relax and let the tension go. Don't do anything for a count of about ten easy breaths. Just pay attention to how it feels.

4. Next, move your attention to your neck and shoulders. Tense them up. Make them rigid. Then relax and let that tension go. Again, wait ten slow breaths to notice how it feels.

5. Now make your arms stiff as boards. When they feel really tense, let the tension go. Again, wait and notice.

6. Pay extra attention to your hands. Make tight fists with them. Then notice how it feels as you allow your hands to relax.

Major Relaxation Techniques

7. Next, tense up all the muscles in your upper torso—your chest and back. Relax that muscle group and again wait for the effect.

8. Moving down your body, tense up the area of your pelvis— your buttocks and the muscles in the lower abdomen and groin areas. Let that tension go and allow about ten breaths for the effect.

9. The next area of your body to focus on is your thighs. Tense them up, then relax them and let the tension ebb away. Allow the ten-breath pause and pay attention to the feeling of relaxation there.

10. Moving down to your lower legs, tense your calves and ankles. Then relax them and let the tension go. Again, pause and enjoy the relief.

11. Finally, tense up your feet and your toes as though they are the feet of a bird, clinging tightly to a branch. Then relax that tension and let it go.

12. Now deepen the relaxation of each part of your body. Without speaking out loud, let your inner voice tell your body what to do.

   • Head and face, relax more deeply.

   • Mouth and tongue, relax more deeply.

   • Neck and shoulders, relax more deeply.

   • Chest and back, relax more deeply.

   • Pelvis and buttocks, relax more deeply.

   • Thighs, relax more deeply.

   • Calves and shins, relax more deeply.

   • Feet and toes, relax more deeply.

13. For a minute or so, remind your neck to relax more and become softer, your shoulders to lengthen and widen, and your back to lengthen and widen. If you are not fully comfortable, gently move around and settle in until you feel at ease.

14. Lie peacefully for the remainder of your twenty minutes and continue to breathe deeply and normally. Each time you inhale, imagine inhaling health and well-being. Each time you exhale, breathe out worry and tension. You may want to imagine warm, healing waves of relaxation passing down your body, from head to toe, each time you exhale. Don't make an effort to think. Just pay attention to your breathing and your body. If a sound you hear or a thought you have interrupts your concentration, just make a mental note of the thought or sound and let it go.

If you're very tired, you may become so relaxed that you fall asleep. As a matter of fact, many people who have difficulty going to sleep at night use this progressive relaxation routine to induce sleep. They simply give themselves permission to go to sleep. The last tension they let go of is the tension of staying awake.

If you want to make sure you don't fall asleep, set an alarm to mark the end of the relaxation period or arrange for someone to tell you when the twenty minutes are up. Another method some people use is to record a musical or spoken wake-up reminder timed twenty minutes from the start of a cassette tape. The cassette player then becomes a custom-tailored alarm clock for your relaxation.

Relaxation Imagery

If you're able to relax fairly quickly without the head-to-toe technique, you may prefer relaxation imagery. You may also want to consider using a combination of the two methods. Start with the tensing and relaxing and silent instructions to your body and then use your imagination to continue and deepen the relaxation.

With relaxation imagery, you use your own plans (made in advance) or recorded instructions or sound effects to guide your imagination through a relaxing fantasy that's like a very vivid daydream. If you find it easy to imagine sights, sounds, and sensations, this may be the most enjoyable relaxation technique for you.

Relaxation fantasies are limited only by your imagination. All that's important is that you choose a fantasy that's calming, relaxing, and peaceful for you. You may want to imagine yourself on a sunlit beach, or in the mountains by a rushing trout stream, or in a "special" room that brings comfort to you. The location can be one that is real or made up, a place you've been or one you've always wanted to visit. The only requirement is that it be a place that brings you peace and relaxation, and that you spend about twenty minutes there to get the full benefit of the fantasy.

One person's relaxing fantasy may be of comfortable solitude, while another's might include real or imaginary people. One person may create the fantasy while lying down, the other in a sitting position. One may plan out everything in advance and go through exactly the same routine each time, while the other prefers to be spontaneous and may even have several fantasy "locations" to go to. Following are the highlights from one person's relaxation fantasy.

I am very relaxed, lying on the fur rug in my living room with my eyes closed. I begin to feel the surface below me warming. I am now lying on the warm sand of a sunlit beach. I decide to just lie there for a few minutes and feel the warmth of the sun and sand. I am alone, and all my worries and cares are far away. The only sound is of the waves breaking on the beach and the occasional cry of a distant seagull. In my imagination, I open my eyes. I see the clear, blue tropical sky. Just the hint of a fluffy white cloud here and there. Far above me, a seagull is flying. I imagine what it must be like to soar unafraid at such a height. I decide to just watch the seagull for a while. After a few minutes, I decide to get up and go for a walk. I walk for some distance, feeling the warm, wet sand under my bare feet. I notice the interesting sea shells on the beach, and there are some hermit crabs. There is a little village down the beach, maybe Polynesian. Nobody seems to be there. Then I see someone in one of the houses. It's my grandmother, and I'm very happy to see her. We hug and have a long talk. I ask her for advice on my career plans, and she tells me to go where my heart tells me. I understand what she means. She reminds me the afternoon will soon be over and it's time for me to return to my place on the sunny beach. We hug again and say goodbye, promising to meet at the village again. I walk slowly back down the beach, feeling calm and reassured. When I get back to my place on the sand, I lie down and again hear the waves on the beach and feel the warm sun on my body. I am back in my living room again, lying on the fur rug. I open my eyes and feel refreshed and ready to return to the work I was doing.

Beautiful scenes and sounds, spontaneous decisions to go exploring, a continuous feeling of serenity and safety, and a conversation with a very wise and treasured person from the past—such were the themes in this person's relaxation fantasy. It's not unusual for the fantasy to include symbolism that suggests new self-insights and solutions to problems. The unconscious mind can be very creative when we're deeply relaxed. What will the themes and places be in your relaxation fantasy? Make some up and let your imagination do the rest.

Major Relaxation Techniques

Your Own Personal Relaxation Tape

Some people find it easier to do their relaxation exercises if they have an assist from something recorded on an audiocassette. A variety of recordings of soothing messages, guided fantasies, relaxing music, and pleasant natural sounds are available in stores. You may want to buy and use some of these, or even make your own relaxation cassette. Some people record their favorite sounds from nature, such as the surf on a quiet beach, a babbling forest stream, or the sound of a gentle rain. Others record their own instructions on relaxing, or their own descriptions of a peaceful fantasy trip.

If you decide to make your own personal relaxation tape, aim for a length of around twenty minutes. That seems to be the minimum duration of relaxation associated with full benefit. If you will be recording natural sounds, make sure the microphone is close enough to the sound source to pick it up clearly, and that there is no irritating background noise (such as traffic) to spoil the effect. If your relaxation tape will include your voice, speak in a calm, gentle, relaxing tone, and speak slowly.

If you make a talking tape, you may find that it takes you several tries to produce one on which your voice sounds calm, reassuring, and relaxing. If so, after a few tries the right vocal sound will come, and there is an added benefit. In learning how to sound calm and relaxed, you are learning how to *be* calm and relaxed!

Don't get the idea that controlling your stress means going around calm and relaxed as if you were tranquilized all the time. There's much excitement, fun, joy, and laughter in a stress-relieved life, and that's the subject of the next chapter.

Chapter Ten

Laughter, Fun, and Stress

"I have seen the enemy and they are us." That bit of folk wisdom from Pogo the possum is absolutely true when it comes to personal stress. In so many ways, we are our own worst enemies. In 1936, when he wrote *How to Win Friends and Influence People,* Dale Carnegie noted that he had never known anyone who died from too much work. Too much worry, he said, was another matter. The message that we need to "lighten up" is an old one.

In *Anatomy of an Illness,* Norman Cousins told the story of fighting back from serious illness through the use of humor and laughter. Soon, patients recovering from heart attacks and cancer surgery were watching Laurel and Hardy movies as part of their therapy. Recoveries were faster and longer-lasting in most cases. Laughter, it turns out, helps mobilize the immune system and reduce stress.

115

Clearly, laughter and light-heartedness are the opposite of DIStress. Studies have even proven laughter to be another stimulant for the production of beta-endorphins, those neurochemicals mentioned in Chapter 5 that are also stimulated by exercise and that increase our tolerance for pain and stress.

Obviously, time for laughter and fun make up a commonsense element of any stress control plan. While we're at it, now would be a good time to develop a healthier sense of humor and learn how to use it as a way of coping with situations that are upsetting and worrisome.

Laughter

Babies first laugh at a game of "cootchie-cootchie" or "upsy-daisey" and at adults making funny faces and silly noises. Little ones laugh at sensations, surprises, and other people laughing too.

As childhood progresses, we laugh at struggles and at how we used to be. We are amused by other people's mistakes and with things that concern other people not being able to do things we have already mastered. The juvenile sense of humor is characterized by silliness, usually of the healthy kind. Look at the style of children's jokes—they crack up at the story about the kid who ran around and around the cracker box because it said "tear around here." (He was silly; he didn't understand.) "Why do elephants wear white sneakers with red polka-dots?" "To hide in cherry trees." "Does it work?" "Sure, did you ever see an elephant in a cherry tree?" The ever-popular "knock-knock" jokes are puns, *plays* on words. Little children's jokes focus on playful silliness and fun.

As time goes on, we learn there are unpleasant and scary things in life. Humor may help cushion those realities. Older kids tell "gross" jokes and squeal with delight at "spook house" humor. About this time, they also begin to laugh *at* other people and make fun of them. Unhealthy humor creeps in.

Adolescence is the time of breaking away from an older generation and of testing limits. Satirical wit that pokes fun at society emerges in adolescence. If it is gentle and not bitter, it becomes a foundation for part of a good adult sense of humor. But adolescence is also the time of "shock" humor and the humor of stereotypes and sometimes bigotry. Many people are amazed when they recall, many years later, the jokes that were funny at a teenage party when no adults were around. So many of those stories are not funny in the least now! We conclude that the humor, if any, was in talking about forbidden subjects and using forbidden words, many of them rough, rude, and disrespectful.

Reckless disrespect is not a good foundation for an adult sense of humor. In adulthood, humor becomes whimsical. It is based on laughing at ourselves and not taking things too seriously. Healthy adult humor brings people together. It doesn't push them apart.

Another type of adult humor isn't based on jokes at all—it's founded in sheer joy. Laughing at a baby's delight over the gift wrappings in the aftermath of a holiday or at a puppy's thrill at dragging around a toy of nearly its own size is the humor of pure joy! The same is true of our laughter when our favorite team scores a touchdown.

There are many things to laugh about in our world, and each laugh relaxes the body, releases stress, fends off distress, and generates endorphins. We work overtime at finding things to worry about. How about spending a few minutes to make a list of things that are worth at least a chuckle? Exercise 17 gives you the opportunity to do just that.

Exercise 17:
I Can Laugh At...

Make a list of things you think are worth a laugh. The list may include your favorite television comedy and a sprinkling of funny movies, but it should also include some things about you and your family, pets, friends, job, and social surroundings. Just start writing and see what you come up with.

_____

_____

_____

_____

_____

_____

_____

_____

_____

_____

_____

_____

_____

_____

_____

_____

Fun

There's an old saying that a wise person can see any theme or event in life as a comedy, a tragedy, an irony, and a love story. We tend to focus on the tragedy, or sometimes the irony, not noticing the first and last items on the list.

Just as there are some things that can be funny to you, there are others that are just plain fun! Laughter is associated with play, as the sounds coming from any playground will assert. But not all play involves laughter. Some is simply pleasure—doing what's natural to you and what you want to do.

The now-famous "executive monkey" studies remind us of the importance of leisurely pleasure. The monkeys were placed in a situation in which they had to make a decision and take action (press a lever whenever a certain light came on) to avoid an unpleasant stimulus. They quickly learned to be very attentive and take the right action. But when they were exposed to the stressful situation continuously without time off for ordinary "monkey activities," they developed ulcers and other stress-related diseases. It was found that they could tolerate the stress if each high-demand period was followed by a reasonable amount of leisure time. Obviously, time for fun is crucial if you're a monkey in the fast lane.

Unfortunately, fun and leisure are often the first things to go as your schedules becomes more hectic. Certainly there are things that are truly urgent in our lives, but as Steven Covey points out in *The 7 Habits of Highly Effective People*, not everything that seems urgent is important, and there are many things in life that are highly important but do not seem urgent at all. If you'll forgive the pun, time to "monkey around" is one of those.

Laughter, Fun, and Stress

Some lucky people find such enjoyment in their fitness sport that it also fills the bill for fun. For most people, though, fitness is pleasant but not high on the fun list. For most people, such a list would instead highlight activities such as going out to dinner, playing cards with friends, browsing at the shopping mall, playing a round of golf, reading a good mystery novel, or playing "catch" with a Labrador retriever. Use Exercise 18 as an opportunity to make a list of *your* current "top ten" pleasurable activities (whether you've been taking time to engage in them or not).

Exercise 18:
My Top Ten Pleasurable Activities List

Write down the ten activities that give you the most pleasure. Include only things that you enjoy—not those you're neutral on but do because someone else likes them.

1. _____
2. _____
3. _____
4. _____
5. _____
6. _____
7. _____
8. _____
9. _____
10. _____

If your list includes some activities you've been missing out on, go back and highlight them with a marker or make a check mark beside them. Now, evaluate whether they're enjoyable enough that you need to work them into your schedule or whether they're really things you'll do only if you get around to it. If they fall into that category, put parentheses ( ) around them. If you decide they aren't important at all, cross them off your list.

Now, use the space below to list the playtime activities from your list that you will take time to enjoy today.

Play for Today

_____

_____

Laughter, Fun, and Stress

If you're going to follow the "executive monkey principle," you need some play activity every day. Maybe a full hour isn't feasible in some busy daily schedules, but a minimum of eight hours of play time over the course of a week is a *must*. And it should be fairly evenly balanced, not all crammed into the weekend. When you find yourself in one of those days when there's no time for fun, rearrange your schedule to allow for at least thirty minutes of pure play.

The final exercise for this chapter is to do what you listed in the "Play for Today" space! Now that's the kind of "homework" nobody complains about.

When you've finished that assignment, you will have covered the basics of relieving or preventing stress through relaxation techniques, diet, health habits, exercise, modification of distressful beliefs, attitude adjustment, assertiveness, laughter, and recreation. Before creating your own personal stress control schedule, make sure you read the next chapter to put it all into perspective.

Chapter Eleven

Beyond Stress Management

As recently as five years ago, what you have read so far would have been considered a "complete" stress management plan. But in the past few years, we've learned more about stress. This, then, is the added chapter "beyond" the mechanics of the typical stress management book or video—it adds *depth of perspective* as the key to stress-free living. The tenets here are by far the simplest, but in many respects also the most difficult in terms of defining what must be done and keeping the resolve to do it. The "beyond stress management" message is short but not small: Live for what you believe in.

The most crippling kind of stress comes from our natural tendency to ignore our values, beliefs, and priorities. Humans have a need for meaning and spirituality in life.

This is not the same thing as needing to embrace a religion or to belong to a church or religious organization: "Spirituality" here means taking care of the needs of the human spirit—that within us which has the potential to be our best self.

In his book *Man's Search for Meaning*, Victor Frankl makes it clear that the belief that life has meaning can be crucial to surviving stressful circumstances. Frankl, who was a prisoner in the Nazi concentration camps of World War II, tells the stories of his survival and of his comrades who did and did not survive. It is impossible to think of a situation more distressful, unfair, dehumanizing, and apparently hopeless. These people were imprisoned without trial, forced to choose hard labor or death while living on insufficient nutrition and without proper medical care. At the same time, they saw friends and loved ones die and be put to death around them daily. Who survived? Frankl says the deciding factor was often a matter of who found a meaning in life and had a pressing reason to survive. He himself was convinced that he couldn't have survived if he hadn't developed a mission to live to write about what he'd been through and what he'd learned.

What do you believe in that will carry you through? Maybe defining this will come easy for you. Maybe not. The rest of this chapter is divided into sections to help you complete the process:

1. Defining what you believe in that is worth living for

2. Using your beliefs to shape your priorities

3. Staying on track and measuring personal growth

What You Believe In

You may be tempted to summarize your beliefs in a simple statement like "I believe in doing what is right" or "I believe in God and the doctrine of the _____ religion." You may have taken your values and beliefs for granted for so long that you've forgotten what they mean in terms of daily living. A short summary statement can be useful, though you may be unable to encompass all (or even the essence) of what you believe in a brief, simple sentence. If your core beliefs don't lend themselves to that sort of documentation, a list of things you do believe in will accomplish what's needed. Exercise 19 will get you started.

Exercise 19:
I Believe In...

To start your list of core beliefs, use an outline or key-word format—sentences aren't necessary. On the lines below, write ten things you believe in. If you run out of items before you get to ten, simply write as many as you can. Here are some examples:

I Believe In...

- Being honest, truthful, and open-minded.
- Putting the common good ahead of my own.
- Fairness and justice.
- Praying to God for guidance every day.
- The importance of the family.
- Helping others whenever possible.
- Being self-supporting and responsible.
- Obeying the law.
- Being kind to others.
- Protecting children and the elderly.

Notice that each of these is action-related. Each articulates something you can do. Now, compose your own list, in any order.

I Believe In...

_____

_____

_____

_____

_____

_____

_____

_____

_____

_____

_____

_____

_____

_____

_____

Now things get a little tougher. Put the things you wrote in priority order, from most important to least important. If you get stuck, it's okay if two or three items "tie" for the same position.

Belief-Based Priorities

Now that you've spelled out what your beliefs are, you can use your list to choose and prioritize your daily activities. For example, if one of your beliefs is being supportive of your children, one of your daily priorities might be to include some time for your children every day. As stated previously, the source of stress for many people is that their priorities and daily activities are out of whack with what they really believe in and value. This gap between what they believe and what they actually do tugs at them—it's a source of stress. Review now your prioritized list of "top ten" beliefs in Exercise 19. Then complete Exercise 20.

Exercise 20:
My Core Belief Priorities

Use the space provided to write yourself a "note" about the things you've been forgetting or neglecting, or maybe the things you want to make sure you continue to include in your life.

In setting my daily priorities and schedule, I need to…

_____

_____

_____

_____

_____

_____

_____

_____

_____

_____

_____

_____

_____

_____

Whether you end up with one reminder note or several, come back to this exercise when you write out your personal stress management plan in Chapter 12. Your reminders will help you include the things that are really important in your life.

Staying on Track

It's easy to start out the day centered on your beliefs and intending to live them to the hilt. The problem is that most days you fall at least a little short of that. The sum of those minor and major slip-ups, those strayings from what you believe in, add up to a mountain of stress. They undermine your self-esteem and pile up guilt. They allow you to hang on to anger and fear. They perpetuate false and inaccurate views of your success or failure.

But there's an easy daily exercise you can perform to help you stay on your values-spiritual track and continue to grow in ways that are most important to you. Twelve-step programs have used a similar method in helping people with just about every compulsion you can think of. It's assisted in kicking habits like alcohol, drugs, overeating, people-pleasing, and living the role of victim. In the process, those who use it become happier and more stress-resistant than many people who never had those problems. The technique is called "taking inventory." It's simple. Every day, at the end of the day, you look at what you truly, deeply believe in and assess just how well you've done at living up to that.

To take inventory, just review your day and see how it measures up to your list of ten valued beliefs. Make written notes if that helps, though most people can do this exercise without a pencil and paper. Give yourself credit for successes, but don't duck the places where you didn't quite make the goal. As a matter of fact, make a note if there's someone you owe an apology, a clarification, or some amend to make up for something you did—or didn't do—during the day. Take care of those shortcomings at the earliest opportunity. End by being grateful for the things you did right and resolve to be more aware, tomorrow, in those areas where improvement is needed.

Now, use Exercise 21 as a sample inventory for the past twenty-four hours or so, just to see what it's like.

Exercise 21:
My Daily Inventory

Use the list of ten valued beliefs you created in Exercise 19 (and your summary statement if you have one) to evaluate the day you just lived through.

Date:_____

Inventory:_____

_____

_____

_____

_____

_____

_____

_____

_____

_____

_____

_____

_____

_____

_____

_____

_____

Include a daily inventory as part of your own personal stress control plan (which you'll design in Chapter 12). After you make your plan, expand the inventory to include how you fared at following your stress control intentions.

One last thing before you go on to create that personalized plan of yours. Your values and beliefs will become more clear to you as you continue to review them and put them into action. The process is called personal or spiritual growth. The time will come when your original list of ten beliefs just won't feel adequate any more. When that day comes, add to it or rewrite it and put the items on the new list in priority order.

All the principles in this book are valuable contributors to DIStress-free living, but the prime principle is expressed in an age-old motto:

TO THINE OWN SELF BE TRUE.

Chapter Twelve

Your Personal Stress Control Plan

"How do I get to Carnegie Hall?"

"Practice, man, practice!"

This old vaudeville line says it all when it comes to controlling stress or making any other life changes. You master what you practice. And as another bit of folk wisdom warns, "If you always do what you always did, you're always going to get what you always got." The goal here is to control stress by changing habits, and doing so requires determination and planning.

Without a plan, it's easy to become disorganized, especially in a matter that has as many facets as controlling stress. This chapter serves to give structure to your stress control intentions and to shape them into a working strategy for a longer, happier life.

Working from the exercises you've completed throughout this book, first fill in each section in the planning form. Then, when you need to schedule certain elements of the plan, use the calendar forms provided or your own daily planner or calendar.

My Personal
Stress-Control Plan

1. My Stress Control Timeouts

In this space, list the techniques or activities from Chapter 2 that you will use as stress-breakers during the day when you feel pressure mounting.

_____ _____

_____

_____

_____

2. My Major Physical Fitness Program

In this space, write the exercise(s) or sport(s) that you chose in Chapter 5 to maintain cardiovascular fitness. Remember, you will schedule a minimum of twenty minutes of this activity three or four times a week.

_____

_____

_____

_____

3. My Off-Day Exercise Program

In this space, list any activities you selected in Chapter 5 to fulfill your need for exercise on days you do not participate in your major physical fitness program. Remember, you will schedule some time for exercise at least six days a week.

_____

_____

_____

_____

Your Personal Stress Control Plan

4. My Positive Attitude Tools

In this space, based on your work in Chapter 7, list the positive thoughts or activities you will use to replace negative thoughts when they intrude.

_____

_____

_____

_____

5. My Immediate Assertiveness Goals

In this space, list any special short-term goals you may have developed while reading Chapter 8.

_____

_____

_____

_____

6. My Major Relaxation Techniques

In Chapter 9, you learned about progressive relaxation and relaxation imagery. Note in this space which technique you plan to use or if you intend to use both. Remember, you will schedule your major relaxation sessions (three to seven per week) when you make your calendar schedule. (They may be scheduled at bedtime as a sleep-inducing activity.)

_____

_____

_____

_____

7. My Plan For Leisure and Play

In Chapter 10, you determined your top-priority play and pleasure activities. List them here. Remember, you will schedule at least eight hours of pure leisure per week, and no calendar day should have less than thirty minutes of "play time."

_____

_____

_____

_____

My Stress Control Schedule

Using the appointment-calendar style pages that follow, schedule a weekly stress control program. (If you use a daily planner that includes spaces for before and after work hours, you may want to use it instead of the pages provided here.)

Schedule stress-control activities for at least one model seven-day week. The following checklist identifies the activities to schedule and the time quotas for each:

_____ MAJOR FITNESS ACTIVITY (20-30 minutes minimum per session, 3-4 times per week)

_____ MINOR EXERCISE SCHEDULE (20 minutes or more per session, to get some exercise at least 6 of 7 days)

_____ MAJOR RELAXATION TECHNIQUES (20 minutes per session, 3 or more days per week)

_____ PURE PLAYTIME ACTIVITY (a total of at least 8 hours a week, never less than 30 minutes per day)

_____ DAILY INVENTORY (every day, at or near bedtime)

_____ NEED FOR SLEEP (whatever you know you need)

	Mon.	Tues.	Wed.	Thurs.	Fri.	Sat./Sun.
5:00						
5:30						
6.00						
6:30						
7:00						
7:30						
8:00						
8:30						
9:00						
9:30						
10:00						
10:30						
11:00						
11:30						
12:00						
12:30						
1:00						
1:30						
2:00						
2:30						
3:00						
3:30						
4:00						
4:30						
5:00						
5:30						
6:00						
6:30						
7:00						
7:30						
8:00						
8:30						
9:00						
9:30						
10:00						
10:30						
11:00						

Your Personal Stress Control Plan

	Mon.	Tues.	Wed.	Thurs.	Fri.	Sat./Sun.
5:00						
5:30						
6.00						
6:30						
7:00						
7:30						
8:00						
8:30						
9:00						
9:30						
10:00						
10:30						
11:00						
11:30						
12:00						
12:30						
1:00						
1:30						
2:00						
2:30						
3:00						
3:30						
4:00						
4:30						
5:00						
5:30						
6:00						
6:30						
7:00						
7:30						
8:00						
8:30						
9:00						
9:30						
10:00						
10:30						
11:00						

	Mon.	Tues.	Wed.	Thurs.	Fri.	Sat./Sun.
5:00						
5:30						
6.00						
6:30						
7:00						
7:30						
8:00						
8:30						
9:00						
9:30						
10:00						
10:30						
11:00						
11:30						
12:00						
12:30						
1:00						
1:30						
2:00						
2:30						
3:00						
3:30						
4:00						
4:30						
5:00						
5:30						
6:00						
6:30						
7:00						
7:30						
8:00						
8:30						
9:00						
9:30						
10:00						
10:30						
11:00						

Your Personal Stress Control Plan

You've made your plan—now work IT! If the plan doesn't work, revise your plan. You may decide, for example, that more pure playtime leisure is more important and effective for you as a regular part of your day than the formal deep relaxation techniques. You may have to cut back to slightly below the recommended quotas on some of the stress-control elements. Keep working on it until you have a plan that works. Then be flexible, but stick with it! If you stop scheduling these important stress control activities, you'll probably find that you stop doing them.

If you have "one of those days" when you can't keep the appointments you made with yourself for healthier living, don't be distressed. Once in awhile those days come along. They're among the things you must learn to accept. Just make sure you get back on your schedule the next day.

Also, don't forget the other parts of the program. There will always be beliefs about day-to-day events that need revising. Life presents a continuing parade of things you must decide whether to accept or change. Negative thoughts will appear from nowhere, requiring thought stopping and replacement. Even your values and core beliefs will mature and change.

Best wishes on a healthier, happier, more productive, DIStress free life!

Afterword: To the Perfectionist

There is one quality that most frequently undermines intentions to control stress. Its name is *perfectionism*.

The perfectionist has an incredible ability to continue pushing him- or herself at just about any activity—work, hobbies, housekeeping, exercise, even stress management. A perfectionist ends up making a competition out of simple pleasures like jogging in the park or swimming laps. Worse yet, it's a competition he or she can never win because the criteria for winning are unattainable.

That leaves the perfectionist only three choices: to push even harder, to stumble on in constant self-disappointment, or to give up and quit trying (often rationalizing that it wasn't really important anyway).

If you have even a glimmer of perfectionism in you, and most of us do, think about the following story:

An amateur musician dreamed of being taught by a great master who was much admired, and whose concerts and recordings were unparalleled in his field. After many years of study, and partly by a turn of fate, the younger player had a chance to study with his idol in a weekend group class at a local college. Though he would spend only a few hours with his role model, he looked forward to the day fervently.

The evening before the class, the master played a concert in the college auditorium and drew a standing ovation from the crowd, which included the younger admirer. The performance was flawless. The amateur player retired to the privacy of his room and practiced late into the night. But with every hour of practice, his anxiety mounted and his performance diminished. Finally he decided, at two in the morning, that he would not solo for the master; he would only play in the ensemble exercises, listening and observing. "I am not," he thought to himself, "good enough to play even the simplest piece in front of this great performer."

On the day of the class, the younger player kept his resolve. As other members of the class struggled with their stage fright and gave ragged renditions of the numbers they had rehearsed, he was glad he had spared himself this embarrassment.

Then the master musician began to play, demonstrating how he had played dozens of songs over several decades—showing the students the techniques and fingerings, all the fine points and tricks of the trade only such a seasoned veteran would know. He played many songs, some of which he had not performed in concert over a career of more than forty years. A few times, with nearly forgotten melodies, he faltered for a moment. Then as the memory of the notes returned, he picked up where he had left off and played the remainder of the tune.

On th day after the seminar, the younger player was practicing in his living room when his wife observed that she had never heard him play so well. "What could you learn in a few hours that could make such a difference?" she asked.

"He makes mistakes," her husband replied. "Don't get me wrong, his concert was flawless as usual. But there in the room with us, playing things we requested that he had not rehearsed, he made a few mistakes."

"Of course he did," replied his wife. "He is a great musician, but he's human. And it would be impossible to have hundreds of selections rehearsed and ready for concert without notice."

"I know," her spouse replied. "But he showed me that the best of them make mistakes, that there is no absolute perfection. And in doing that, he gave me permission to make mistakes. He also taught me what to do when you make one. If the mistake is of little consequence, you laugh about it. If it is something more important, you do it again until you get it right. Then, you relax and enjoy doing what you do, and you become much better at it…and sometimes very soon."

Afterword: To the Perfectionist

Bibliography and Suggested Reading

Alberti, Robert E., and Michael L. Emmons. *Your Perfect Right*. San Luis Obispo, CA: Impact Publishers, 1995.

American Psychiatric Association. *Diagnostic and Statistical Manual of Mental Disorders, (4th ed.)*. Washington, DC: American Psychiatric Association, 1994.

Bandler, Richard, and John Grinder. *The Structure of Magic: A Book About Languages and Therapy (vol. 1)*. Palo Alto, CA: Science and Behavior Books, 1975.

Bandler, Richard, and John Grinder. *Frogs into Princes: A Neuro Linguistic Programming*. Moab, UT: Real People Press, 1979.

Beck, Aaron T., A.J. Rush, B.F. Shaw, and G. Emery. *Cognitive Therapy for Depression*. New York: Guilford Press, 1979.

Benson, Herbert. *The Relaxation Response*. New York: William Morrow, 1975.

Bradshaw, John. *Healing the Shame That Binds You*. Deerfield Beach, FL: Health Communications, 1988.

Burns, David D. *Feeling Good: The New Mood Therapy*. New York: Morrow Company, 1980.

Burns, David D. *The Feeling Good Handbook: Using the New Mood Therapy in Everyday Life*. New York: Morrow Company, 1989.

Carnegie, Dale. *How to Stop Worrying and Start Living*. New York: Simon & Schuster, 1984.

Carnegie, Dale. *How to Win Friends and Influence People*. New York: Simon & Schuster, 1981.

Chapman, Elwood N. *Life Is an Attitude*. Menlo Park, CA: Crisp Publications, 1992.

Cousins, Norman. *Anatomy of an Illness as Perceived by the Patient: Reflections on Healing and Regeneration*. New York: W.W. Norton, 1979.

Covey, Stephen R. *The Seven Habits of Highly Effective People*. New York: Simon & Schuster, 1989.

Dyer, Wayne. *Your Sacred Self: Making the Decision to Be Free*. New York: Harper Collins, 1995.

Ellis, Albert, and Robert A. Harper. *A New Guide to Rational Living*. Englewood Cliffs, NJ: Prentice-Hall, 1975.

Fairfield Poley, Michelle. *A Winning Attitude: How to Develop Your Most Important Asset!* Mission, KS: SkillPath Publications, 1989.

Frankl, Viktor Emil. *Man's Search for Meaning: An Introduction to Logotherapy*. New York: Simon & Schuster, 1962.

Friedman, Paul. *How to Deal With Difficult People*. Mission, KS: SkillPath Publications, 1989.

Maultsby, Maxie C., Jr., and Allie Hendrix. *You and Your Emotions.* Lexington, KY: University of Kentucky Medical Center, 1974.

Peck, M. Scott. *The Road Less Traveled: A New Psychology of Love, Traditional Values, and Spiritual Growth.* New York: Simon & Schuster, 1978.

Pelletier, Kenneth. *Sound Mind, Sound Body: A New Model for Lifelong Health.* New York: Simon & Schuster, 1994.

Satir, Virginia. *Peoplemaking.* Palo Alto, CA: Science & Behavior Books, 1972.

Selye, Hans. *Stress Without Distress.* Philadelphia, PA: J.B. Lippincot, 1974.

Schroeder, Joel, and Ruth Schroeder. *Putting Anger to Work for You!* Mission, KS: SkillPath Publications, 1995.

Schutz, Will. *The Truth Option: A Practical Technology for Human Affairs.* Berkley, CA: Ten Speed Press, 1984.

Smith, Manuel. *When I Say No I Feel Guilty: How to Cope—Using the Skills of Systemic Assertive Therapy.* New York: Bantam Books, 1975.

Tinbergen, Niko, ed. *Animal Behavior.* The Life Nature Library. New York: Time-Life Books, 1965.

Audiocassettes

Canfield, Jack. *How to Build High Self-Esteem.* Chicago, IL: Nightingale Conant, 1989.

Sullivan, Nancy. *Stress Management for Women.* Mission, KS: SkillPath Publications, 1993.

Available From SkillPath Publications

Self-Study Sourcebooks

Climbing the Corporate Ladder: What You Need to Know and Do to Be a Promotable Person
  by Barbara Pachter and Marjorie Brody

Coping With Supervisory Nightmares: 12 Common Nightmares of Leadership and What You Can Do
  About Them *by Michael and Deborah Singer Dobson*

Defeating Procrastination: 52 Fail-Safe Tips for Keeping Time on Your Side
  by Marlene Caroselli, Ed.D.

Discovering Your Purpose *by Ivy Haley*

Going for the Gold: Winning the Gold Medal for Financial Independence *by Lesley D. Bissett, CFP*

Having Something to Say When You Have to Say Something: The Art of Organizing Your Presentation
  by Randy Horn

Info-Flood: How to Swim in a Sea of Information Without Going Under *by Marlene Caroselli, Ed.D.*

The Innovative Secretary *by Marlene Caroselli, Ed.D.*

Letters & Memos: Just Like That! *by Dave Davies*

Mastering the Art of Communication: Your Keys to Developing a More Effective Personal Style
  by Michelle Fairfield Poley

Organized for Success! 95 Tips for Taking Control of Your Time, Your Space, and Your Life
  by Nanci McGraw

A Passion to Lead! How to Develop Your Natural Leadership Ability *by Michael Plumstead*

P.E.R.S.U.A.D.E.: Communication Strategies That Move People to Action *by Marlene Caroselli, Ed.D.*

Productivity Power: 250 Great Ideas for Being More Productive *by Jim Temme*

Promoting Yourself: 50 Ways to Increase Your Prestige, Power, and Paycheck
  by Marlene Caroselli, Ed.D.

Proof Positive: How to Find Errors Before They Embarrass You *by Karen L. Anderson*

Risk-Taking: 50 Ways to Turn Risks Into Rewards *by Marlene Caroselli, Ed.D. and David Harris*

Speak Up and Stand Out: How to Make Effective Presentations *by Nanci McGraw*

Stress Control: How You Can Find Relief From Life's Daily Stress *by Steve Bell*

The Technical Writer's Guide *by Robert McGraw*

Total Quality Customer Service: How to Make It Your Way of Life *by Jim Temme*

Write It Right! A Guide for Clear and Correct Writing *by Richard Andersen and Helene Hinis*

Your Total Communication Image *by Janet Signe Olson, Ph.D.*

Handbooks

The ABC's of Empowered Teams: Building Blocks for Success *by Mark Towers*

Assert Yourself! Developing Power-Packed Communication Skills to Make Your Points Clearly, Confidently, and Persuasively *by Lisa Contini*

Breaking the Ice: How to Improve Your On-the-Spot Communication Skills *by Deborah Shouse*

The Care and Keeping of Customers: A Treasury of Facts, Tips, and Proven Techniques for Keeping Your Customers Coming BACK! *by Roy Lantz*

Challenging Change: Five Steps for Dealing With Change *by Holly DeForest and Mary Steinberg*

Dynamic Delegation: A Manager's Guide for Active Empowerment *by Mark Towers*

Every Woman's Guide to Career Success *by Denise M. Dudley*

Grammar? No Problem! *by Dave Davies*

Great Openings and Closings: 28 Ways to Launch and Land Your Presentations With Punch, Power, and Pizazz *by Mari Pat Varga*

Hiring and Firing: What Every Manager Needs to Know *by Marlene Caroselli, Ed.D. with Laura Wyeth, Ms.Ed.*

How to Be a More Effective Group Communicator: Finding Your Role and Boosting Your Confidence in Group Situations *by Deborah Shouse*

How to Deal With Difficult People *by Paul Friedman*

Learning to Laugh at Work: The Power of Humor in the Workplace *by Robert McGraw*

Making Your Mark: How to Develop a Personal Marketing Plan for Becoming More Visible and More Appreciated at Work *by Deborah Shouse*

Meetings That Work *by Marlene Caroselli, Ed.D.*

The Mentoring Advantage: How to Help Your Career Soar to New Heights *by Pam Grout*

Minding Your Business Manners: Etiquette Tips for Presenting Yourself Professionally in Every Business Situation *by Marjorie Brody and Barbara Pachter*

Misspeller's Guide *by Joel and Ruth Schroeder*

Motivation in the Workplace: How to Motivate Workers to Peak Performance and Productivity *by Barbara Fielder*

NameTags Plus: Games You Can Play When People Don't Know What to Say *by Deborah Shouse*

Networking: How to Creatively Tap Your People Resources *by Colleen Clarke*

New & Improved! 25 Ways to Be More Creative and More Effective *by Pam Grout*

Power Write! A Practical Guide to Words That Work *by Helene Hinis*

The Power of Positivity: Eighty ways to energize your life *by Joel and Ruth Schroeder*

Putting Anger to Work For You *by Ruth and Joel Schroeder*

Reinventing Your Self: 28 Strategies for Coping With Change *by Mark Towers*

Saying "No" to Negativity: How to Manage Negativity in Yourself, Your Boss, and Your Co-Workers *by Zoie Kaye*

The Supervisor's Guide: The Everyday Guide to Coordinating People and Tasks *by Jerry Brown and Denise Dudley, Ph.D.*

Taking Charge: A Personal Guide to Managing Projects and Priorities *by Michal E. Feder*

Treasure Hunt: 10 Stepping Stones to a New and More Confident You! *by Pam Grout*

A Winning Attitude: How to Develop Your Most Important Asset! *by Michelle Fairfield Poley*

For more information, call 1-800-873-7545.

Notes

Notes

Notes

Notes

Notes

Notes

Notes

Notes